# Where There's a
# Will
# There's a Way

# WHERE THERE'S A
# Will
# THERE'S A WAY

*Or, All I Really Need to Know
I Learned from Shakespeare*

LAURIE MAGUIRE, PH.D.

A PERIGEE BOOK

**A PERIGEE BOOK**
**Published by the Penguin Group**
**Penguin Group (USA) Inc.**
**375 Hudson Street, New York, New York 10014, USA**

Penguin Group (Canada), 90 Eglinton Avenue East, Suite 700, Toronto, Ontario M4P 2Y3, Canada (a division of Pearson Penguin Canada Inc.)
Penguin Books Ltd., 80 Strand, London WC2R 0RL, England
Penguin Group Ireland, 25 St. Stephen's Green, Dublin 2, Ireland (a division of Penguin Books Ltd.)
Penguin Group (Australia), 250 Camberwell Road, Camberwell, Victoria 3124, Australia (a division of Pearson Australia Group Pty. Ltd.)
Penguin Books India Pvt. Ltd., 11 Community Centre, Panchsheel Park, New Delhi—110 017, India
Penguin Group (NZ), Cnr. Airborne and Rosedale Roads, Albany, Auckland 1310, New Zealand (a division of Pearson New Zealand Ltd.)
Penguin Books (South Africa) (Pty.) Ltd., 24 Sturdee Avenue, Rosebank, Johannesburg 2196, South Africa

Penguin Books Ltd., Registered Offices: 80 Strand, London WC2R 0RL, England

While the author has made every effort to provide accurate telephone numbers and Internet addresses at the time of publication, neither the publisher nor the author assumes any responsibility for errors, or for changes that occur after publication. Further, the publisher does not have any control over and does not assume any responsibility for author or third-party websites or their content.

First edition: November 2006

Library of Congress Cataloging-in-Publication Data

Maguire, Laurie E.
  Where there's a will there's a way : or, all I really need to know I learned from Shakespeare / Laurie Maguire.
     p. cm.
  ISBN 0-399-53294-3
  1. Conduct of life. 2. Self-help techniques. 3. Life skills. 4. Shakespeare, William, 1564–1616.
5. Psychology and literature. I. Title.

BJ1581.2.M34 2006
158—dc22

                                                                                        2006018175

PRINTED IN THE UNITED STATES OF AMERICA

10   9   8   7   6   5   4   3   2   1

Most Perigee Books are available at special quantity discounts for bulk purchases for sales promotions, premiums, fundraising or educational use. Special books, or book excerpts, can also be created to fit specific needs. For details, write: Special Markets, The Berkley Publishing Group, 375 Hudson Street, New York, New York 10014.

*For the triumvirate of wonderful women*
*Dympna Callaghan*
*Anne Coldiron*
*Rebecca Whiting*

# CONTENTS

| | | |
|---|---|---:|
| | *Acknowledgments* | IX |
| Prologue | LEARNING TO "SEE BETTER" | 1 |
| One | IDENTITY | 9 |
| Two | FAMILY | 29 |
| Three | FRIENDS | 43 |
| Four | THE BATTLE OF THE SEXES: COMEDY | 55 |
| Five | THE BATTLE OF THE SEXES: TRAGEDY | 73 |
| Six | UNREQUITED LOVE | 83 |
| Seven | ACCEPTANCE | 95 |
| Eight | ANGER | 105 |
| Nine | JEALOUSY | 121 |
| Ten | POSITIVE THINKING | 135 |
| Eleven | FORGIVENESS | 147 |
| Twelve | TAKING RISKS | 159 |
| Thirteen | MATURITY | 167 |
| Fourteen | LOSS | 183 |
| Epilogue | WHERE THERE'S A WILL | 197 |
| | *Relevant Reading* | 205 |

# ACKNOWLEDGMENTS

It is a pleasure to thank all those who have contributed to this book. In Washington, D.C.: Thomas L. Berger, Dympna Callaghan, Anne Coldiron, Debra Drummond, Ann Rosalind Jones, Claire MacDonald, Anne and James Maguire, Rachel Miola, Gail Kern Paster, William Sherman, Adam Staerck, Peter Stallybrass, Joe Tarantolo, Paul Yachnin, Georgianna Ziegler. In Ottawa: David Carlson, Donald Childs, Laura Denker. In London: Katie Aston, Angelika Percy, Elizabeth Schafer, Rebecca Whiting. In Oxford: Sharon Achinstein, Katherine Duncan-Jones, Elisabeth Dutton, Sos Eltis, Kristine Krug, Candia McWilliam, Danielle Sered, Emma Smith, Martine Stewart, Gill Woods, Blair Worden.

In the world of publishing I wish to thank Catherine Clarke and all at Felicity Bryan Literary Agency in Oxford; Emma Parry at Fletcher Parry in New York; Anne McDermid at Anne McDermid and Associates in Toronto; and John Duff and Helen Reeves at Penguin. I am grateful to Farrar, Straus and Giroux for permission to quote Philip Larkin's "This Be the Verse" from *Collected Poems*, ed.

Anthony Thwaite (1988). Some of the observations in this book appeared in an earlier form in *Studying Shakespeare* (Oxford: Blackwell, 2004). For permission to reprint and revise them, I am grateful to Blackwell Publishing.

My deepest gratitude goes to those companions on the journey: Dympna Callaghan, Anne Coldiron, and Rebecca Whiting at the beginning, and Peter Friend who joined along the way.

## CITATIONS

All Shakespeare quotations are taken from the *Riverside Shakespeare* (Boston: Houghton Mifflin, 1997). Where necessary I have modernized distracting archaic spellings.

# Prologue

## LEARNING TO "SEE BETTER"

It doesn't much matter which edition of Shakespeare you read. If you're an athlete, you might like the Oxford *Complete Works* (2005) or the *Riverside Shakespeare* (1997); they can double as arm weights in aerobics classes and save you the cost of a gym membership. If you're a smoker, you might like the *Norton Shakespeare* (1997), based on the *Oxford Shakespeare*: it's printed on such thin paper that in an emergency you can roll your own. (And if you can have a cigar called Hamlet, why not a cigarette called Shakespeare?) If your back pocket functions as your briefcase, you might like the single-volume paperbacks published by Signet or Penguin. Or you can mix and match: I carry the one-dollar Thrift edition *Sonnets* (Dover Press) in my handbag but have a tower of doorstop omnibus editions on the floor of my study at home.

Whatever series you buy, you will have at your fingertips strategies for survival and success.

Each of Shakespeare's plays depicts a human predicament and attempts a solution. The predicaments are personal, political, social (in other words: human), and the solutions, whether comically successful or tragically ill timed, come from characters whose motivations and mistakes are recognizably contemporary. In reading these plays we encounter life's predicaments and characters' strategies for dealing with them. In other words, Shakespeare's plays offer life coaching.

This is a book about life. It is also a book about Shakespeare. Or perhaps that should be the other way round: Shakespeare first, life second? Whatever (as they say in America); what you will, or as you like it (as Shakespeare says). It doesn't really matter because in my book (where book is a metaphor for a code of conduct, a guiding principle) the two are the same.

I didn't always think this way. In fact I have been trained not to think this way. Literary criticism is increasingly sophisticated, and it finds increasingly sophisticated ways of reading Shakespeare. For the last several decades it has not been fashionable for professional Shakespearians to talk about Shakespeare characters as if they were real people living real lives. (They are not, of course; but, as critic Robert N. Watson points out, *we* are.) Academics talk about epistemology and representation and semiotics and *différance* and liminality and cultural positions, and these are all things worth talking about. But so is Shakespeare as life, and as a guide to life—as I found out in 1999.

Occasionally we have an annus horribilis. 1999 was mine. I broke my heart and had a delayed adolescence. My investments plummeted and I went down with pneumonia. To cap it all, my cleaning lady threw out the handwritten manuscript of my new book. Because I happened to be in the United States at the time, and because the United States is the land of self-help philosophy, I did what you would expect. I read my way through the entire self-help section of my local bookstore. And that's when I realized that I had read it all before: in Shakespeare.

I had always known Shakespeare was a cultural icon. Now I understood he was a self-help guru. I had my very own life coach.

My father was dying; I read *Hamlet.* No, not the play about assassination but the one about a young man who can't get over his father's death. That's what *Hamlet* is about. I had a tempestuous Latin boyfriend so I studied Shakespeare's bad boys: Petruchio, Troilus, Diomedes. I was approaching forty; I read *Antony and Cleopatra* for examples of midlife career and romance. Everything I needed to know in life I learned from Shakespeare.

Shakespeare's situations are as familiar to human beings and the human heart today as they were four hundred years ago. You may not have been shipwrecked in Illyria, but that is not what *Twelfth Night* is about. It is about loving someone who doesn't love you back; it is about being obsessed and behaving excessively. If you have ever pondered your employer's strategies, your enemy's motives, your friend's childhood, your colleague's errors, your own insecurities, or your partner's faults (even your partner's insecurities, or your *own* faults!) you have participated in a Shakespeare play, whether as actor, audience, or critic.

Actors will tell you that they approach Shakespeare's plays first through character and situation; audiences respond first to character and situation; the daily drama of our lives also revolves around the palpable emotional realities of character and situation. With Shakespeare, as with life, we're simply trying to get our heads round the thoughts and nature of the woman who rejects a man, the guy who pursues a girl, the father who misunderstands a daughter, the politician who takes a country to war . . .

Thus, Shakespeare is not just a poet and playwright: he's a psychologist. In bookstores and libraries Shakespeare appears in the drama section, the literature section, and sometimes even in the poetry section. He should also be in the self-help section. In today's school curriculum crisis, where Shakespeare's relevance is increasingly questioned and attacked, we overlook this crucial fact: Shakespeare's plays show us human lives in all their perplexing and unpredictable variety. They show us choices, good and bad; they show us predicaments, tragic and comic; they show us characters, complex and shallow. They show us ourselves.

This is not to claim, as Harold Bloom does, that Shakespeare *invented* the human. He didn't. But he understood it. Shakespeare's plays show us our own situations writ large, our own character writ large. It is this understanding of the interaction between character and situation that makes Shakespeare a psychologist before the field of psychology existed as a profession. Our lives are simply stories whose conclusions are not yet scripted, and we are characters in our own dramas.

We live our lives through stories. When we ask our partner or roommate, "How was your day?" what we are really saying is: "Tell me the story of your day." Stories shape experience for us, help us process the world.

Some stories get told over and over again. The story of Eve in Christian tradition replays the story of Pandora in pagan tradition: both women allow curiosity to get the better of them, Eve eating the forbidden apple and Pandora opening the sealed box. Both stories are attempts to explain how evil got into the world, implicit warnings to us not to repeat these mistakes. But these are a specific subgenre of story: myth. Myths *prescribe* whereas stories *explore*. Whereas myths tell us how we must live, stories (in the words of critic Carolyn Heilbrun) tell "how we might learn to live." And no storyteller explores more astutely how we might live than Shakespeare.

In *The Gift of Fear*, Gavin de Becker's brilliant and compassionate handbook for survival, de Becker advises us all to approach situations from someone else's point of view. De Becker is a psychologist who works as a security advisor to high-risk clients such as Hollywood stars and U.S. government officials. He points out that when we are confronted with out-of-character behavior (usually in the form of unexpected violence) we respond with incredulity: "Who could have predicted it?" "Who would have imagined it?" These are the typical responses of family and friends on the TV news. As the French surrealist playwright Eugène Ionesco wrote, "You can only predict things after they have happened." But for de Becker, no action is ever unpredictable or out of character. *Everything* is imaginable—and hence predictable—if only we learn to approach things from another's point of view. And prediction is the first step to prevention.

To see things from another's point of view requires imagination. It takes practice. It is difficult. Sometimes it is impossible until one has experienced the same situation. Youth cannot imagine old age—until it ages. Happiness cannot imagine misery—until caught in the same despair. When King Lear puts his daughters through a love test, asking them to quantify their emotions, Cordelia refuses to cooperate. She sees things only from her stance—youthful, principled, inflexibly honest. Would she have behaved this way if, *for one moment*, she had seen things from her elderly father's point of view? If she had seen that beneath the bizarre test lay an old man's fear of being unloved? It's a sobering thought that we might create tragedy simply by being unimaginative.

But the good news is we can avoid tragedy by exercising our imagination.

I have been practicing the Shakespeare/de Becker approach in my own life for several years. No situation is too trivial. A few years ago my husband and I were trying to buy a house whose historic interest meant that any renovations were subject to strict restrictions. It transpired that the vendor's multiple improvements had never received the required approval; this made the property a legal liability. Negotiations dragged on for months with the vendor becoming more and more defensive. Perplexed by her intransigence, I tried to see things from her point of view. Immediately, the situation became clear. She thought she had created a "home"; the authorities thought she had behaved like a vandal. She had "improved" her house; the authorities were implicitly criticizing her taste. She was an innocent widow; the authorities made her feel criminal. Had we failed to complete this purchase it would not have been a personal tragedy. But the clash between our surveyor's letter-of-the-law attitude and the seller's domestic emotional investment was not so far from the standoff between Cordelia's ruthless application of principle and Lear's emotional vulnerability (indeed, in *A Thousand Acres*, Jane Smiley's Pulitzer Prize–winning update of *King Lear*, Smiley rewrites the Cordelia character as a lawyer). Seeing things from the vendor's point of view resulted in a change of rhetorical tactic (and a happy ending for all concerned).

Stories, then, present us with roles we might not yet imagine and outcomes we might not be able to envisage. "See better," Kent's injunction to Lear, is not just a moral injunction to a morally blind monarch. It is an encouragement to us all; it is a constant refrain in this book. (What can we see behind the angry person? One who feels frustrated at his or her lack of control? What can we see behind the jealous partner? A vulnerable person permanently afraid of loss?) To see better is to see ourselves better, to see the world better, to imagine causes and consequences. And Shakespeare's stories enable us to try out other people's point of view, to see the world from a different perspective, to live other people's stories.

Like all good storytellers, like all good life coaches, Shakespeare doesn't legislate. He invites us to explore our emotions and judgments. He asks questions; he gives suggestions; he offers possibilities; he comforts and encourages; he coaches. Ultimately he helps us take control of the plot in our own lives; he helps us discover ourselves.

# One

## IDENTITY

*Who is it that can tell me who I am?*

—*King Lear*

"Know thyself" is the great message of life and literature, from the Delphi oracle to Shakespeare, from Greek tragedy to weekly therapy sessions. This might sound like a cliché, but clichés are simply truths with which we've become bored.

Knowing yourself, finding yourself, being yourself is simple in theory but hard in practice. "Of course I believe in free will. What choice do I have?" I don't know who said this but the theological paradox encapsulates a tension equally applicable to personal identity: the tension between what is determined for us (the expectations and baggage we inherit from family, from society) and what is determined by us (the choices we make). Who we are or how we see ourselves begins before we're even aware of the process. Some of the influences on us are barely perceptible; they're in the air that we breathe. Being yourself is the subject, explicit and implicit, of most of the chapters in this book. This chapter is specifically about the multiple and hidden pressures that influence our developing selves, the stuff that comes from society or parents or friends.

These are large topics (parents and friends even get chapters to themselves in this book). Shakespeare consistently intertwines them, however, by focusing on the personal name—the verbal marker of identity that is given us the moment we enter the world. How does our name influence our sense of personal identity?

Margaret Atwood raises this question in her short story "Gertrude Talks Back." Gertrude tells her son, "I always thought it was a mistake calling you Hamlet. I mean, what kind of name is that for a young boy? . . . I wanted to call you George." Implicit in her comic confession is the notion that Hamlet's life might have been very different had he been called something else. The fifteen-year-old narrator of Mark Haddon's award-winning novel, *The Curious Incident of the Dog in the Night-Time*, negotiates this issue from a related angle as he contemplates his name, Christopher:

> My name . . . means *carrying Christ* and it comes from the Greek words χριστος (which means *Jesus Christ*) and φερειν and it was the name given to St. Christopher because he carried Jesus Christ across a river . . . Mother used to say that it meant Christopher was a nice name because it was a story about being kind and helpful, but I do not want my name to mean a story about being kind and helpful. I want my name to mean me.

What does it mean for a "name to mean me"? This is Shakespeare's most recurrent question in his exploration of identity.

I should begin by confessing that I have a vested interest in this topic. As names go, "Laurie Maguire" is a mean trick to play on a baby. In America, where Lauries and Loris abound, my first name wouldn't be a problem. For me, growing up in Scotland, however, it was a headache: it's a boy's name, it's an abbreviation, it's a surname. It's not a name to give a girl. A girl named Laurie is as ridiculous as a boy named Sue.

Compound "Laurie" with "Maguire"—spelled the Irish rather than the Scottish way—and you have a recipe for disaster. (And why should my grandfather spell his name M*a*guire when all his relatives were M*c*Guire? Because his father had one too many celebratory whiskies on his way to register the birth, that's why.)

At the start of every school year, in every subject, throughout primary and secondary school, I was called upon to spell my name. How I hated being singled out in a class of Annes and Elizabeths, Smiths and Browns. How I identified with Groucho Marx's character in *A Night in Casablanca*: "No, that's not my name, I'm just breaking it in for a friend." A name is more than a label; it's a character, a shorthand, a set of associations. It's your identity: it is who you are.

And if you don't like it, your name is not merely a word; it's a sentence.

My name was awkward and attention-calling. But the baggage that goes with names can be unequivocally positive. When I met my husband, Peter Friend, I was enchanted by the associations of his name: a rock, a supporter. *Bonum nomen, bonum omen:* good name, good omen. Peter Friend boded well, and I wasn't the only one to think so. When the BBC did a series of TV programs about the hospital where Peter was a consultant surgeon, a TV reviewer pounced with delight on his name and that of his colleague, Chris Constant. If you're going to be ill, she observed, you want to be looked after by doctors with names like Peter Friend and Chris Constant.

Reading names in this way—that is, seeing an association between an individual's label and his or her identity—was an interpretive reflex to Elizabethans. (It's called "onomancy.") It didn't matter if you believed that names *created* identity (that a "Theophilus" would grow up to be a "lover of god") or that names simply *reflected* identity ("Septimus" is always going to be a seventh son), the point was that names had meaning. It was up to the individual to fulfill that meaning or ignore it. The Renaissance belief in onomancy led to a number of books designed to help parents and godparents choose an inspiring and appropriate name for a newborn and to help others live up to (if good) or refute (if bad) the meanings of their names.

The French author Montaigne (1533–92), whose essays were translated into English in 1603, gives an example of the kind of effect good names could have. A licentious young man, preparing to have sex with a young woman, happened to ask her name. On being told it was Mary he was immediately overcome by the depravity of his intended action to the bearer of a sacred name; he not only dressed and left but founded a convent dedicated to the Virgin Mary.

In Shakespeare's day it was still customary for godparents to choose the names of their godchildren. The baptismal ceremony was a ceremony for children and godparents (the mother was not present, having not yet been "churched" after childbirth). Whether godparents chose the newborn's name in consultation with the parents is not clear. Since godparents often gave their own names to their godchildren—as Hamnet and Judith Sadler did to Shakespeare's twins, Hamnet and Judith—the parents could indirectly register their choice of children's name through their choice of godparents. In any case, baptismal practice changed during the late sixteenth and seventeenth centuries with more and more parents assuming responsibility for naming their offspring. Nonetheless, as late as 1696 a distressed father and neighbors prevailed upon a vicar to rebaptize a child "Thomas" after the baby's godfather had christened him "Job." To a society that viewed names as a form of behavioral predestination, Job hardly augured well.

All of a sudden I feel a whole lot better about being called Laurie. It means victorious—from the Latin laurel, the garland of bay leaves awarded to winners.

∼

The play in which Shakespeare offers the most sustained investigation of name and identity is *Romeo and Juliet*. In this play the young lovers try to break away from the identity imposed by their families and the Veronese society of which they are prominent members. Shakespeare encapsulates these social pressures—behavioral expectations, family pressures, tradition, inheritance—in two words: the surnames Montague and Capulet.

Juliet poses the play's key question, "What's in a name?" in soliloquy after the ball at her father's house. Her family, the Capulets, are engaged in a long-standing feud with another Veronese family, the Montagues. Despite the Montagues' conspicuous and deliberate exclusion from the Capulets' guest list, young Romeo Montague and his friends gate-crash the Capulet party. He and Juliet meet, converse, and fall in love, ignorant of each other's name or family. At the end of the ball they independently discover each other's parentage, and at the beginning of the next scene Juliet, in her first moment of privacy, reflects on names, namelessness, and identity. It is this dilemma that occupies her famous soliloquy: "O Romeo, Romeo, wherefore art thou Romeo? / Deny thy father and refuse thy name" (2.2.33–34).

However, the name whose value she questions first is not the given name but the surname, Montague/Capulet. The history of hatred attached to these surnames makes it impossible for Romeo (a Montague) and Juliet (a Capulet) to love each other.

Juliet argues that Romeo is an individual independent of his surname, and so his identity and actions cannot be programmed by his surname. Montague is simply a label, not a material part of identity: it is "nor hand nor foot / Nor arm nor face, nor any other part / Belonging to a man" (2.2.40–42). Thus, "a rose / By any other word would smell as sweet" (2.2.43–44).

From here she moves to the first name and toys with the idea of a Romeo who is neither a Montague nor a Romeo. Both names are irrelevant, she says, because Romeo would be himself whatever he's called (2.2.45–47). Unknown to Juliet, Romeo stands below her window, eavesdropping on this fantasy of linguistic freedom and when he reveals his presence, Juliet asks in alarm, "What man art thou that . . . stumblest on my counsel" (that is, Who's there?). The question is now impossible to answer as Romeo realizes: "By a name / I know not how to tell thee who I am" (2.2.53–54). Humans need names.

The name may begin as a label ("*how* to tell thee who I am"), but it quickly becomes a part of our identity ("*who* I am"). Juliet uses a sartorial image ("doff thy name"), implying that a name is external and detachable, as easy to remove as a cap, but a few scenes later Romeo shows us how integral names are. Having accidentally killed Juliet's cousin Tybalt, he shelters in Friar Lawrence's cell, weeping in despair. When Juliet's nurse arrives, she explains that Juliet collapses whenever Romeo's name is mentioned. Romeo turns to the friar and pleads, "tell me, / In what vile part of this anatomy / Doth my name lodge? Tell me, that I may sack / The hateful mansion" (3.3.105–8). His offer is not just a grand rhetorical gesture, a removal of the offensive name, but an overture to suicide as the friar's next line reveals: "Hold thy desperate hand" (3.3.108). Clearly Romeo has his dagger poised to cut out his name. But he and his name are one.

When I took up my job in Oxford, the IT staff made an error

with my name so all my e-mails were titled, "From: Lauren Maguire." My inbox quickly filled with hurt e-mails from friends I'd known for twenty years: "I never knew your name was Lauren," they wrote. Not to know someone's name is not to know them as an individual, as the Bastard in *King John* realizes. He plans to insult acquaintances by getting their name wrong: "if his name be George, I'll call him Peter" (1.1.185). For better or for worse, our name is related to our identity.

The same holds true of surname changes. I am surely not the only woman to have experienced an identity crisis when my husband expected me to take his surname. To him this was a personal gift; to me it was unbearable loss. It's not that I was particularly fond of my surname—quite the contrary!—but it and I had been together a long time. I had embroidered it on my gym-shoe bag; I had corrected people's spelling of it endlessly. I was attached to it (literally).

The inseparability of name and identity is seen repeatedly throughout *Romeo and Juliet* in both minor and major characters. The kitchen servants are aptly named Gradgrind and Potpan. The musicians all have musical names: Simon Catling (a lute string), Hugh Rebeck (a violin), and James Soundpost (a peg on the bridge of a stringed instrument). Juliet's name means "born in July"; her nurse tells us that she was born on Lammas Eve (31 July). And Romeo, whose name means "pilgrim," fulfils his name when he meets Juliet. He holds her hand, justifying this presumptuous advance on the grounds that palm to palm is a pilgrim's action; he offers his lips as "two blushing pilgrims" ready to pay homage.

In loving Juliet, Romeo is living up to his name, is fulfilling his destiny, and has become himself; the pilgrim has found his shrine, reached his object of veneration. To "doff" his name would therefore mean not to love Juliet, not to be Romeo, to deny his identity. Shedding a name is not the simple action Juliet imagines. We see this today in the pop world with "The Artist Formerly Known as Prince." He can only deny his name by invoking it; a name is for life. (And so in 2005 he reverted to "Prince.")

Perhaps Romeo should answer Juliet's question as to who's there with, "The suitor formerly known as Romeo."

We no longer assign names with the expectation that the name's origin will reflect or influence the bearer: Kirk Douglas need not be a Scotsman who lives near a church ("kirk") and a dark blue river (Gaelic "douglas"). Nonetheless, the popularity of baby name books, complete with lists of origins, literary precedents, and historical fashions, suggests a degree of residual if temporary onomancy. And parents' acknowledgment that they chose a name because they liked its associations (with relatives, friends, or celebrities) is simply a diluted variant of etymology (the name still has an origin). If our naming practices are no longer demonstrably motivated, however, our reading practices are, at least if *Reader's Digest* columns of apt names and professions are anything to go by: Les Plack, a dentist; Mr. Flood, a urologist; Shearer's, a barber's shop. In 2001 a Brazilian father was prevented by the authorities from naming his son Osama bin Laden; nine years earlier he had been prevented from naming a son Saddam Hussein. Legal intervention was deemed necessary because there is an association between the person's label and his or her identity. To name a child Hitler or Saddam Hussein today is as ominous as christening a child Job was in the Renaissance. We assume that the child's identity will be formed by their name.

Throughout the canon Shakespeare is alert to the significance of his characters' names. The name of the fool in *Twelfth*

*Night*, Feste, aptly reflects his profession, as does that of his Puritan opponent, Malvolio (ill will). Consider the pacifist *Ben*volio (goodwill) in *Romeo and Juliet*. The soothsayer who prophesies harmony at the end of *Cymbeline* is aptly named Philharmonus (love of harmony). In *2 Henry IV* Falstaff requests Pistol's exit with an anachronistic pun on his name: "Discharge yourself of our company Pistol" (2.4.137). In *As You Like It* both Celia and Rosalind choose relevant disguise names ("something that hath a reference to my state"; 1.3.127), Aliena (the estranged one) and Ganymede (Jove's epicene page), as does Imogen in *Cymbeline*, whose alias, Fidele, is remarked approvingly by her new master: "Thy name well fits thy faith; thy faith thy name" (4.2.381).

But although Shakespeare's plays repeatedly offer a *relation* between name and identity, they protest against the concept of name as *destiny*. In *1 Henry IV*, written a few years after *Romeo and Juliet*, the minor characters Samson Stockfish and Francis Feeble do not have the profession or trait that their names imply. These characters are, as critic Anne Barton argues, "celebrations of human freedom, self-conscious assertions that even fictional characters can defy their names." Shakespeare says: your family can name you, but they cannot tell you who you are.

In 2002 Victoria and David Beckham named their second son Romeo, prompting speculation about the name's significance for the couple. British rapper? Brazilian footballer? Italian designer? The Beckhams disclaimed any association, insisting that the name had no meaning; the couple just liked it. That may be. But all names have meaning whether we want them to or not. The Beckhams were naive in denying their child's name meaning; the Shakespeare play with which the Beckham baby will inevitably be associated makes this point all too well.

What we do with these associations is up to us. You can change your name (as aspiring celebrities often do, feeling hampered by "ordinary" names). You can use an awkward name to develop a thick skin (successful people have often "overcome" their name). You can give your child an auspicious name. But we must never make the mistake of thinking that what we are called equals who we are.

Romeo's names pull in opposite directions. To be a Montague means to hate all Capulets, but to be Romeo means to be a pilgrim. Romeo can worship Juliet or hate her. But he has a choice; his behavior is not determined by his names. He is who he chooses to be.

Shakespeare's interest in the problem of personal names is part of his interest in the problem of the label generally. We live our life through labels; we react to labels. We identify ourselves with our professional label: architect, teacher, homemaker. We define ourselves and others with adjectival labels: kind, organized, confused, flexible, caring. We have denominational titles and allegiances: Protestant, Catholic, Jew, Arab, Republican, Democrat, Socialist, Tory. We have black and white labels, literally: black, white. But these labels always limit. If I change religion or political party or personal name, am I a different person? In his book *Awareness*, the Jesuit writer Tony de Mello says that "the important thing is to drop the labels . . . What do I mean by labels? Every label you can conceive of except perhaps that of human being. I am a human being. Fair enough; doesn't say very much. But when you say 'I am successful,' that's crazy. Success is not part of the 'I.'" As Julie Andrews's Maria trilled in *The Sound of Music*, "me, a name I call myself." The only identity we have is "I" or "me"; all other labels are externally imposed.

For de Mello, the mistake we make in life is identifying ourself with our label. "We spend so much of our lives reacting to

labels, our own and others'. We identify the labels with the 'I.'"
De Mello reminds us that Niagara Falls is composed of constantly changing water but is known by a stable name: Niagara Falls. The name is for convenience; let us not make the mistake of equating the identity with the label.

We need only consider the etymology of the word "label" to see the wisdom of this caveat. "Label" comes from the Old French word meaning a strip of cloth or linen, a ribbon that was attached to a document as a supplement. (This gives us our modern meaning of label as a sticker or piece of cardboard attached to an envelope or parcel.) A person's label—their name—is likewise an attachment, a supplement; it is an adjunct to the person and not the person him/herself. How society labels us—white, middle class, salesperson, failure, success, Montague, Capulet—is not who we are.

In the opening scene of *Romeo and Juliet*, the Montague and Capulet servants draw weapons and fight. It is a reflex action: Capulets are conditioned to fight when they see a Montague, and vice versa. They see only the label. It is this that the young lovers protest against.

But dropping labels is hard to do. Why did I feel the need to identify de Mello as "the Jesuit writer"? Or as a "writer" of any kind? Why not just call him Tony de Mello? Yet to call him by his name is still to use a label, and although Juliet fantasizes about anonymity, it is hardly a practical solution.

The solution is not to drop the label but to see beyond it. Shakespeare wants us to see the individual, not the label. He stresses this throughout the canon but dramatizes it most obviously in the partner play to *Romeo and Juliet*: *Othello*. Like *Romeo and Juliet*, *Othello* is a love tragedy and it shares with *Romeo and Juliet* imagery of light and dark, white and black. But what was metaphor in the early love tragedy is now literal. Desdemona sees beyond the surface, however, sees beyond the label "black": "I saw Othello's visage in his mind" (1.3.252). So does the Duke: "Your son-in-law is far more fair than black" (1.3.290). "Black" is a label attached to Othello, just as "Othello" is a label attached to him. But neither label represents who he "is." As Juliet says, "So Romeo would, were he not Romeo call'd, / Retain that dear perfection which he owes [owns] / Without that title" (2.2.45–47). In other words, Romeo—or Othello—would be who he is irrespective of his label.

~

Last year I went to a costume party where the instruction was to come as a literary character. I plundered the garden for laurel leaves and went as Ovid's Daphne, metamorphosed into a tree. "Ah," said one of my students, "you have come as your name." I hadn't meant to but I had. I had come as myself. I had become myself. There's no getting away from names.

But maybe there is. The laurel leaves were an adornment, attachments to my dress, my earrings, my belt, my hair. They were a "supplement," a "label"; as such they could be removed. I had achieved Juliet's wish: in the course of the evening I "doffed" my name.

~

The self, as Stephen Greenblatt and other cultural critics have shown, was a new category in Elizabethan England. Medieval man's and woman's identity had been defined in relation to community and to God; identity was communal, not individual. The "humanist" movement of the sixteenth century, as the term indicates, placed the individual in the foreground, and it did so in a positively secular way: the medieval concept of a God-centered universe was replaced by one based on humans and their potential.

This was not a change of theology but a change of emphasis: if God made the earth for humans, self-improvement was a mark of respect for God. (This anthropocentric approach is open to criticism, of course; but I am summarizing history, not deconstructing it.) Man's potential as an individual was therefore to be developed.

The word "self" as a noun meaning one's own nature or personality first entered the English language in a sonnet by Edmund Spenser, published in 1595: "my self, my inward self I mean" (*Amoretti* 45). You can see the newness of the term in that Spenser has to explain it: "my inward self I mean." Prior to this, "self" had been used reflexively to intensify a personal pronoun (as in "I did it myself") or adjectivally (as in "the selfsame thing"). But as a noun the self became a substance, a category: in short, an individual.

It is no coincidence that the emergence of the self as a category coincides with the emergence of Elizabethan lyric poetry. Lyric poetry's raison d'être is the exploration of intense forms of individuality, of personal experience: love, anguish, suffering. *Romeo and Juliet* (1595) is one of Shakespeare's most lyrical plays. It was written the same year as Spenser's sonnet and is heavily indebted to the 1590s vogue for love poetry: its originality consists in presenting in dramatic form the intense personal feelings that had so far only been attempted in love poetry. In act 1, Romeo exclaims: "Tut, I have lost myself, I am not here: / This is not Romeo, he's some other where" (1.1.197–98). To lose oneself presupposes that one has a self to lose. We take such an assumption for granted today so the enormity of this statement in 1595 is easily overlooked.

The self begins early. I recently visited a friend with a week-old baby. She apologized on behalf of her son: "He's not himself today." Already he had a self not to be! At the other end of the spectrum I read an interview with an octogenarian film director who, when asked about old age, said, "What I miss most is myself."

Sometimes Shakespeare's plays invoke a concept of selfhood that is simply synonymous with being human, as when Duke Senior in *As You Like It*, exiled in the Forest of Arden, contrasts his previously pampered court life with his current exposure to the elements. He prefers the latter: "these are counsellors / That feelingly [that is, physically, tangibly] persuade me what I am" (2.1.10–11). What I am: human. He opposes the honest counsel of the elements ("*This* is no flattery") to the sycophancy of courtiers (who presumably persuade him that what he is is more than human: a duke).

At other times Shakespeare examines the self at moments of specific cultural pressure: when a black man marries a white woman (*Othello*), when a man's best friend takes a wife (*The Merchant of Venice, Much Ado About Nothing*), when a nun is sexually harassed and blackmailed (*Measure for Measure*), when a country invades another (*Henry V*), when two children of feuding families fall in love (*Romeo and Juliet*). But even here, the category of general humanity overlaps with the moment of localized investigation. Lear's general identity crisis ("who is it that can tell me who I am?"; 1.4.230) is precipitated by two specific personal crises—retirement and his daughter's marriage (as we shall see in chapter 2).

The entire Shakespeare canon is a course in Finding Oneself 101. In *The Comedy of Errors* Adriana tries to find her sense of self within marriage. For her, identity is dependent on another person: her husband. If her husband does not behave like a husband, she says, if he does not pay attention to her, if he visits prostitutes, if he frowns at her, she cannot feel like a wife. Like

Antipholus of Syracuse in the same play, who seeks his lost twin brother in order to find himself, Adriana feels her identity incomplete without another human being. For her, what it means to be "me" means to be part of "us."

But Adriana's is only one of multiple approaches in this play to the question of personal identity. The farcical confusions of this plot, with *two* sets of identical twins and the repeated mistaking of identity, raise large questions about what "being me" might mean: how do we know who we are if someone else looks like us? If someone else treats us as someone we are not? If someone else has the same name as us?

Duplicate names are the problem encountered by Troilus and Cressida. As the couple pledge love and fidelity to each other, their vision of living happily ever after is haunted by the specter of their names. Troilus and Cressida were the lovers of a popular medieval story famous for its unhappy ending in which Cressida betrayed Troilus. (The story was so famous that the characters' names became synonyms for their associated behaviors, Cressida being used as a shorthand for the faithless woman and Troilus as a standard of loyalty.)

Shakespeare's play of *Troilus and Cressida* repeatedly offers a fractured vision of selfhood—"this is and is not Cressid"—as the characters try to forge an identity independent of the tragic story with which their names are associated. The play uses a literary situation to exemplify a predicament we all face: trying to be author of our own story, trying to be ourselves, independent of the expectations and pressures placed on us by family, friends, society. "As truth's authentic author to be cited" says Troilus (3.2.181), meaning he wants to begin his story here and now, not to live someone else's script. His reference is both literal (he is aware that he is a literary character rather than himself) and metaphorical: we all want to be the authentic author of our own story.

Shakespeare uses the same metaphor of authorship later in the canon, in the tragedy *Coriolanus*, when the hero talks about a man being "author of himself." In this play Shakespeare asks how a man can be author of himself when his family has decided what path his life is to take. How difficult is it for us to find our identity within others' pre-scripted narratives?

In Coriolanus's case, the author pre-scripting his narrative is his mother. Volumnia has molded her son's martial personality and takes pride in the fact: when he was a child she, "considering how honor would become such a person, . . . was pleas'd to let him seek danger where he was like to find fame. To a cruel war I sent him." She boasts that if she had a dozen sons she would rather lose eleven in battle than have one die in peace. Volumnia has carefully and deliberately created a fighting machine, an animal, an unsocialized and antisocial creature: "a thing," a "lonely dragon," "an engine," "a sword," "a dog." As one character in the play says, Coriolanus "has been bred i' th'wars / Since 'a [he] could draw a sword" (3.1.318–19).

Coriolanus does not have a father but he has a father figure, the elder statesman Menenius, whose attitude parallels Volumnia's. In act 2 Menenius shares Volumnia's perverse delight in anticipating the wounds Coriolanus might receive in battle. Both live vicariously through Coriolanus.

As a military leader Coriolanus is most at ease on the battlefield, but in the middle of the play he has to perform Rome's electioneering equivalent of kissing babies for the cameras. To be elected consul, he must wear the "napless vesture of humility" (an unluxurious fabric symbolizing his humble attitude), display his war wounds in public, and ask "kindly" for votes. This he does, briefly and awkwardly, then immediately asks his advisors "May I change these garments? . . . That I'll straight do; and, *knowing myself again*, / Repair to th' Senate-house" (2.3.146–48, my emphasis).

He can't wait to get out of the performance outfit and mode. To perform politically in public means to be someone other than he is.

Exactly who Coriolanus is, however, is far from clear to me. The different political factions in the play present him differently at different times, depending on their immediate needs: he is variously a military machine, enemy number one, a flatterer, proud, self-seeking and self-interested, patriotic and selfless. Coriolanus is to Rome what tofu is to recipes: an ingredient that takes on a different flavor according to what you need it for. Coriolanus has no identity beyond that ascribed to him by others.

His name says it all. It is an honorific, an additional name given to him after his conquest at the battle of Corioles. He derives his identity from a military achievement, an external event.

This might be OK (although I don't think Anthony de Mello, above, would think it so) since his professional identity is something he has chosen. But is it? Coriolanus illustrates the difficulty of following your family's agenda—in his case, his mother's—rather than your own. His military achievements fulfill Volumnia's ambition rather than his own: "My mother, you wot [know] well / My hazards still [always] have been your solace" (4.1.27–28). In other words, he exists to please her.

Volumnia is clearly ambitious, aggressive, and militaristic. These are highly Roman, if unfeminine, virtues. Volumnia solves the contradiction by dedicating her son to Rome. Thus we see a chain reaction in societal pressure. Coriolanus's young son already acts like his father (destroying butterflies rather than Rome's enemies) because he copies his father's attitudes and actions. Coriolanus acts the way he does because he has internalized his mother's values. Volumnia acts the way she does because she has internalized Rome's values. Biology has an equivalent of this phenomenon: stem cells. What makes multipotent stem cells become specialized cells? Environment. Put a stem cell in a kidney and it will become a kidney cell. Put a stem cell in a brain and it will become a brain cell. The plebeians, patricians, tribunes, the Volscians, Volumnia all view and use Coriolanus as a stem cell, making him become what their environment dictates. In these conditions Coriolanus hasn't a hope of being "author of himself."

I have been subject neither to political manipulation nor to militaristic brainwashing nor to the vicarious ambitions of a dominant mother. Nonetheless Coriolanus's attempts to please others, to allow himself to be what others want him to be, strike a chord in my own life. Like many children in my generation I was conditioned to behave deferentially to adults, to sublimate the child's "me" in deference to the adult's "me." Adults of all ranks—shop assistants, teachers, neighbors—embodied authority and were not to be questioned or contradicted. The procedure was simple: you nodded, you smiled, you agreed. A desire to please and egregious acquiescence were the hallmarks of the polite child. The child's needs or desires as an independent being—as "me"—were paid scant attention.

This applied in all areas, great and small. Taken for an afternoon visit to one of my father's colleagues, I was presented with a cup of milky tea. I loathe milk. Even as a child I drank tea black with lemon. Aghast at the color of the drink in front of me, I hesitated. My father's eyebrows performed acrobatics, cuing my dutiful response: "Thank you, that will be lovely."

One cup of milky tea is hardly a tragedy. More problematic was my first eye test at the age of thirteen. Optometrists' tests proceed by trial and rejection. The optometrist places a series of lenses in front of your eyes and asks for a comparative reaction. "Is this better?" "Now this?" "Or this?" To a child trained in adult-pleasing responses there could only be one answer to such questions: an appreciative "yes, thank you." When I collected my first pair of glasses two weeks later, all horizontal surfaces—the kitchen table, the ironing board, the floor—presented themselves at an angle of forty-five degrees.

It is hard to move from total self-abnegation as a child to autonomy or self-assertion as an adult. Coriolanus is so conditioned to be what his mother wants him to be, what Rome needs him to be, that he has little chance of being otherwise. Thank goodness he didn't need glasses.

Shakespeare continually explores identity but he does not tell us how to be ourselves. No one can tell us how to be ourselves. Therapists do not prescribe; they unlock. Shakespeare simply shows us the dangers of not being ourselves; he shows the tragedies of societal pressures (in this chapter: the pressures of Veronese families and the Roman state) that do not allow people to be themselves. And in these ways he unlocks the gate to our own individual and different paths to self-discovery, self-knowledge, and self-assertion.

Cordelia in *King Lear* does not have any problems with self-knowledge. In the opening of her play she remains true to herself, refusing to cooperate with the absurd love test staged by her father to "prove" which of his three daughters loves him most. Playing the game on her own terms, remaining stubbornly and literally honest in a situation that demands reassurance (telling your old, vulnerable father how much you love him) she triggers tragedy. With her terse and bluntly honest responses, she would have been better off answering questions at my optometrist's office. (And given the play's recurrent use of optical imagery, maybe she thought she was!)

The point is: how can we be ourselves while still being sensitive to the needs of others? And how can we be sensitive to the

needs of others without losing ourselves? How
answer truthfully at the optometrist's and dij
scene 1 of *King Lear*? To consider these questio
look in detail at one of our most formative influenc
tially fraught relationships: the family. That is the s
next chapter.

# Two

# FAMILY

*A little more than kin, and less than kind.*

—*Hamlet*

A few years ago I was having coffee in the common room with three male colleagues who were "losing" their children (male and female) to college life. New men, hands-on fathers and sensitive carers to a T, they shared their personal/parental confusion. In launching their children in the world, they were facing a new definition of themselves. They had created capable, independent beings; in so doing they had made themselves (semi-)redundant. No longer parents to children, they were parents to adults. They no longer knew who they were. The quiet houses were welcome havens but also constant reminders of absence. One colleague had an eight-year-old who was grieving over her brother's departure. Another, having delivered his last daughter to university, noticed the lack of conversational buffers between himself and his wife at meals. He found himself combing his hair and changing his shirt before dinner. "It's like going on a date," he said. "I feel obliged to be interesting. I get nervous."

It had never occurred to me that my own departure for

university might have been felt as a loss or have changed family dynamics (between my parents, between them and my sister). But in retrospect, change was inevitable: the relationship between parent and offspring was now triangular, not two sets of two. My sister was suddenly (but even more confusingly, temporarily) the older daughter, an only daughter. Definitions of self and selves were instantly changed.

Three weeks after the common-room conversation, one of my colleagues expressed delight when his daughter rang home for a special recipe. "I'm still useful," he said. "I feel needed."

The need of the parent to be needed is a theme that underpins *King Lear*. When children are young, parents always feel needed; children rely on them for food, for clothing, for attention, for love. Parents of teenagers still feel needed, if only for money! But things change as children become adults and take on an existence outside the family. When Lear's youngest daughter embarks on marriage, the event changes family dynamics, making Lear feel vulnerable. When daughters get married today, their marriage does not change family life in the way it once did since they have almost certainly already left home: for college, for job opportunities, for travel. Nonetheless, families still experience Lear's emotional disruption and ontological dilemma. ("Ontology" is the science of being. It is a science we all pursue every day!) When teenagers leave home for college, family, parental, and sibling identity is destabilized.

One of the things that makes family life difficult is that there are different constituencies with different needs. The status quo is constantly changing: children become teenagers, teenagers become adults, parents become grandparents. Prodigal sons return, dutiful daughters rebel. Concepts of "selfhood" are in constant flux. (We see this in its most basic fashion every morning when we open our closets. We think we are asking, "What shall I wear today?"; in fact we are asking, "Who do I feel like being today?")

We are different people at different times in our lives. We are encouraged to believe that life is about destinations; in fact, it is about definitions, about who we are at different times. This is true from a very young age: a new baby turns an only child into a big brother or sister, a younger child into a middle child. As relative positions change, as hierarchical positions change, so do we.

In *King Lear* different generations negotiate changing definitions of who they are. At first the play seems to present a general, universally applicable question about identity. Lear's tormented question, "who is it that can tell me who I am?" (1.4.230), is one we might all pose of ourselves. In his attempts to answer this question Lear moves further and further from civilization: from the court and the throne room to the heath and the hovel, stripping off his clothes in his attempt to find quintessential humanity: "the thing itself," "unaccommodated man."

But Lear's general category of "man" is complicated by subdivision. He is not just a generic "man" but a specific kind of man: a king and a father. And these subdivisions are themselves further subdividable: the king is on the point of retirement, the father is about to lose his youngest daughter in marriage. Lear's general identity crisis is thus related to specific personal crises. He is trying to find himself at two transitional moments, moments when his sense of self is being renegotiated.

In moving from king to ex-king, from leader to nonleader, Lear experiences the difficulty most of us encounter when negotiating a transfer from our identity as externally derived, bestowed by profession ("*what* I am"), to identity as something internal ("*who* I am"). Lear is confronting the problem we explored in chapter 1, the problem of the label. One of the first questions we ask strangers at cocktail parties is, "What do you do?" because it gives us a superficial answer to the question we really want to ask, which is: "Who are you?"

It is this ontological difficulty that underlies the hybrid form of retirement chosen by Lear. He gives up "power, / Pre-eminence, and all the large effects / That troop with majesty"; he confers "all cares and business from our age . . . on younger strengths"; but he retains "the name, and all th'addition [honors and prerogatives] to a king" (1.1.130–32, 39–40, 136). He wants authority without responsibility. (Today he'd be a consultant.) But monarchy doesn't have the kind of position envisaged by Lear.

Eddie George (the governor of the bank of England, not the NFL football player!) said that retirement is the movement from *Who's Who* to "Who's He?" That is a transitional crisis indeed. But Lear's transition to retirement is exacerbated by another transitional crisis. The play's first scene presents the marriage negotiations for Cordelia, the last of Lear's daughters to leave home. What is Lear's identity as a *parent* when his daughters have flown the nest? The play juxtaposes questions of professional identity with questions of parental identity. The question Lear later poses to Goneril—"Are you our daughter?" (1.4.218)— is just another way (a sarcastic way) of asking, "Am I a father?"

The family crisis raises a further symbiotic difficulty, not that between self and society but that between *our* sense of our self and *others'* sense of their selves. If Lear's daughters do not act like daughters—that is, if they reject him and deny him hospitality, if they deny their filial identity—does he lose his identity as a father?

～

What do things look like from the children's point of view in *King Lear*? To answer that we need to think about events before the play, and the way they are presented in the first scene. *King Lear*'s first scene introduces us to the patriarchs of *two* families: King Lear and the earl of Gloucester. (Theme of the first scene? *Meet the Parents*.)

Edmund, the illegitimate son of the earl of Gloucester, is making a rare public appearance. He has been abroad for nine years and we are told that he will soon be sent away again. Clearly Edmund is an embarrassing peccadillo in Gloucester's past, although the earl tells us that he has become inured to Edmund's existence: "I have so often blush'd to acknowledge him, that now I am braz'd to't" (1.1.10–11). Gloucester introduces Edmund to a courtier, the earl of Kent, with a salacious "nudge nudge, wink wink" attitude toward his son's illegitimate origins: "Though this knave came something saucily to the world before he was sent for, yet was his mother fair, there was good sport at his making, and the whoreson must be acknowl-edg'd" (1.1.21–24). In other words: "his mother was good-looking and good in bed, and so I'd better take responsibility for the bastard."

Gloucester is entitled to have such sentiments but there is another, more decorous way, of expressing them, and Kent offers it: "I cannot wish the fault undone, the issue of it being so proper" (1.1.17–18). Why can't Gloucester speak this way, at least in his son's presence?

It's an odd opening and shows a side of Gloucester that we don't see subsequently. In the rest of the play Gloucester is the victim, a vulnerable old man. Edmund is the villain.

A slighting parental tone like this is perhaps enough to explain Edmund's creative malevolence in the play as he plots to disinherit his legitimate brother. However, Edmund's malignancy moves from the personal and pragmatic (a desire to inherit lands) to the vicarious and the vengeful: he silently acquiesces in the three plots to torture his father, to murder Lear, and to murder Lear's youngest daughter, Cordelia. While the plot for his brother's land may be an understandable, if immoral, consequence of illegitimate exclusion, the escalating violence is not. What are we to make of this?

Let us fast-forward to the end of the play when Edmund is dying. Several plot details remain to be untied, and Edmund holds the answers: he knows the whereabouts of Lear and Cordelia, and is the only person who knows that his written command for the murder of both is still in the hands of the assassin who is even now on his way to carry out the murders. (Edmund has authority as coleader of the military forces against Lear.) Albany asks Edmund for information but, before he can answer, both are distracted by the dead bodies of Lear's eldest daughters, Goneril and Regan, who are carried on stage. Edmund exclaims, "Yet Edmund was belov'd!" (5.3.240). This reference is to his love affairs with both of the dead women. Although Edmund has been involved with both women simultaneously, this is a moment of pathos, not a declaration of triumph. It is a statement of pride and gratitude. In Edmund's sentence we hear not the macho boast of the Lothario but the desperate cry of the child seeking and needing love, seeking and needing proof that he is lovable. At the moment of death (his lovers' and his own imminent death) Edmund can look back with satisfaction on the fact that he has received (and so been deemed worthy of ) emotional attention.

This need of the child-adult Edmund is also the need of the child-adult Lear, and, in the play's opening scene, Lear takes steps to legislate love. He sets up a public love test in which each of his three daughters has to compete with her siblings in declaring the greatest amount of love for her father: "Tell me, my daughters / . . . Which of you shall we say doth love us most" (1.1.48, 51). The winner will be awarded the largest third of Lear's kingdom as prize.

The contest is a disaster from the start, for the simple and obvious reason that love is neither legislatable nor quantifiable. "There's beggary in the love that can be reckon'd," says Antony in a later Shakespeare tragedy, *Antony and Cleopatra* (1.1.15). Antony knows what Lear does not: any love that can be measured must be scant indeed. Lear's problem throughout the play is that he tries to measure love. Goneril later offers hospitality to fifty of Lear's knights whereas Regan offers accommodation to only twenty-five. Lear therefore concludes that Goneril's love is twice Regan's. Cordelia sees the problems in measuring love in this way and accordingly refuses to play the game. She has nothing to say as proof of her love and is consequently disinherited by her father.

Cordelia's pointed refusal to cooperate is justifiable philosophically: love cannot be reduced to games or measurements or tests or proofs. But her behavior is not justifiable emotionally. If she were to think about the episode from her father's point of view (the tactic we explored in the prologue: "see better," Cordelia), she would see that behind the love test lies an old man's fear and vulnerability: a fear of being old and unloved. At a time when Lear is relinquishing his public position and parting with his last daughter he questions his worth as a human being. Uncertain about his value he creates a situation that will literally declare his worth. One does not have to be a king and patriarch to experience this predicament. In life, when we have finished playing leading parts of whatever kind, we try to direct the new actors. But attempts at control are really expressions of fear.

The terms of the love test are designed to sabotage Cordelia's marriage. Either way, Lear will keep her and her love. If Cordelia declares she loves her father "all," she downplays the emotional bond in marriage. If she doesn't make this declaration, she will be disinherited, which makes her unmarriageable. This is indeed what happens. Burgundy has no interest in a dowry-less Cordelia; it is only the fairy-tale devotion of the king of France ("she is herself a dowry"; 1.1.241) that salvages the proceedings.

The love test choreographed by Lear caters to two vulnerable points in his sense of himself (as a retiring professional and as a father). What it requires, then, is not a statement of truth but a gesture of reassurance. Technically Cordelia is correct when she offers the logical response that she can't love her father more than her future husband ("Sure I shall never marry like my sisters, / To love my father all"; 1.1.103–4), but emotionally she misses the point completely. As a result, Lear, like Edmund, experiences a dark night of the soul and wanders through the play feeling betrayed and unloved.

*Feeling* unloved is as damaging as *being* unloved. It is patently obvious to us that Cordelia loves Lear. But what good is that if Lear does not know it, or if he comes to know it only too late?

In her first response to Lear, Cordelia says that she loves her father "According to my bond [duty], no more nor less" (1.1.93). Lear takes this as an insult. However in the next act he invokes the "bond of childhood" as the highest tribute a child can pay to a parent. Correcting Regan's filial disrespect, he reminds her "Thou better know'st / The offices of nature, *bond* of childhood, / Effects of courtesy, *dues* of gratitude" (2.4.177–79; my emphasis).

In family contexts throughout the Shakespeare canon, "bond" is a compliment, a measure of devotion. It is the bedrock of family relations. In *As You Like It* the love of the cousins Rosalind and Celia is so great that it exceeds "the natural bond of sisters" (1.2.276). In *All's Well That Ends Well* the countess of

Rossillion describes her natural affection for her son: "my love hath in't a bond" (1.3.188). In *King Lear* Gloucester's barometers of moral disaster include "the bond crack'd 'twixt son and father" (1.2.109). In the Shakespeare canon *everyone* prefers bonds!

Bill Bryson recounts a wonderful story from his early days in England when he saw a shop sign saying FAMILY BUTCHER; he went in and asked, "How much to do mine?" The anecdote is designed to illustrate linguistic and cultural difference. But it contains a transcultural reality—at some time some of us have wanted, just for a moment, a family butcher in this (mistaken) sense.

Tension is part of family life. Alan Bennett writes, "I have never understood this liking for war. It panders to instincts already well catered for in any respectable domestic establishment." But family tensions needn't create a dysfunctional family. Shakespeare says: go home tonight and tell your family that you love them.

Parents have a raw deal in literature as in life. They get blamed for everything. I have a retired colleague whose daughter, aged forty, still behaves like a petulant teenager, unable to forgive him for leaving home when she was twelve. She punishes him regularly with rudeness, caustic comments, demands, snide comparisons. But as John-Roger and Peter McWilliams point out in *Life 101*, there comes a point when we have to acknowledge that we are adults, in control of our own lives. "Your childhood is over. You are in charge of your life now. You can't blame the past, or anyone in the past, for what you do today. Even if you can formulate a convincing argument, it does you no good at all. It's past." They offer the useful example of glass and gravity; we break a glass but we don't blame gravity, although without gravity the glass would not have fallen. "Your childhood is like gravity. It was what it was. Your life today is the glass. Handle it with care.

If it breaks, it's nobody's fault. Clean up the mess and get another glass from the cupboard."

Parents simply do what they think best. In *Coriolanus* Volumnia forces her son into politics and sacrifices him to the state to fulfill both her own ambitions and those of the state. Titus Andronicus also privileges state over family. (It's a Roman thing.) Most Shakespeare parents are well meaning if shortsighted in their parental attitudes and actions. Gertrude cannot anticipate the effect her remarriage will have on her grieving son, Hamlet; Egeus in *A Midsummer Night's Dream* and Capulet in *Romeo and Juliet* behave typically for the time in insisting their daughter marry the husband they have chosen.

Children don't come with instruction manuals. Parents learn on the job. And depending on the personality of the child (for "personality" read the "selfhood with which it is born"), the job may not match the job description the parent imagined. As the Restoration poet John Wilmot revealed, "Before I got married, I had six theories about bringing up children; now I have six children and no theories."

One of my friends has never forgotten the pain of being sent to boarding school at the age of eight. He felt deeply and inconsolably rejected, a feeling that has stayed with him through life; but his parents were simply doing what middle-class English parents felt best for their children. (A therapist friend of mine says, sadly, "Boarding schools are very good—good for business.") The British journalist Katharine Whitehorn observes, "Mothers go on getting blamed until they're eighty but shouldn't take it personally."

So how does one get over the pain of family life? Shakespeare's advice is the advice he gives elsewhere for romantic relationships, the advice he gives consistently for all relationships. Try to prevent problems by trying out the other person's point of view. "See better." Accept the person/parent with all their irritations, flaws, and eccentricities: you cannot change them, but you can change how you react to them. And if damage has already been done that renders this advice belated, forgive. Forgiveness is such a powerful tool in Shakespeare that in this book I give it a chapter all to itself (chapter 11). Forgiveness does not let a flawed or abusive parent off the hook but it liberates the forgiving son or daughter from the cycle of self-perpetuating anger and pain.

Unquestionably Lear has been a difficult father and a flawed human being. Goneril reveals that her father has always had a favorite daughter, Cordelia, a preference Lear has already confirmed in public: "I loved her most" (1.1.123). Lear has poor judgment, Goneril says, and even in the prime of life he was impetuous; his irascibility is a "long-ingraff'd [deep-rooted] condition," now compounded by the "unruly waywardness" of old age (1.1.297–98). Regan agrees that he "hath ever but slenderly known himself " (1.1.293–94). Even allowing for bias and resentment, there must be some basis to these complaints. In the 1976 Royal Shakespeare Company production, Judi Dench's Regan had a stammer that only affected her in the presence of her father. This wonderfully subtle addition hinted at deep-seated family tensions.

Forgiving a parent like Lear cannot erase the past. But it erases the current pain of holding on to the past. By resenting or hating our parents we give them control over our life. With forgiveness we take back control. And we must do this before the parent dies because once he or she has gone, guilt will be added to the emotions. Freedom from negative feelings will then be much harder to obtain.

In act 4 we meet a changed Cordelia. She has shed the self-righteous arrogance of act 1. She bears no grudge against her father for his misjudgment of her, for disinheriting her, for refusing further contact with her. Instead she kneels to him and asks for his blessing. He reminds her that she has cause to hate him for what he has done. She denies this in a simple monosyllabic repetition: "No cause, no cause" (4.7.74).

No cause? She has plenty. But she chooses to ignore them; she chooses to forgive.

Lear picks up this sentiment in act 5. Imagining his life in prison with Cordelia, he says: "When thou dost ask me blessing, I'll kneel down / And ask of thee forgiveness" (5.3.10–11). He tacitly acknowledges his responsibility. He asks for forgiveness—the forgiveness that she has already granted.

∽

From Lear to Larkin: "they fuck you up, your mum and dad. / They may not mean to, but they do." Larkin's poem ("This Be the Verse") offers an empathetic view of parents: "But they were fucked up in their turn / By fools in old-style hats and coats" (as we saw in the first chapter of this book, this is Volumnia's situation, conditioned in her turn by Roman values, which she passes on to her son). Nonetheless Larkin's poem ends pessimistically: "Man hands on misery to man. / It deepens like a coastal shelf. / Get out as early as you can, / And don't have any kids yourself." King George V had an alternative to Larkin's solution of childlessness. He advised a do-as-you-were-done-to retaliation: "My father was frightened of his mother. I was frightened of my father, and I'm damned well going to make sure that my children are frightened of me."

Shakespeare offers a better strategy than Larkin's or George V's, as we saw above: tell your family that you love them. And he has a backup plan lest the declaration of love come too late:

forgive them. Forgiveness does not undo damage, but it frees you from being disempowered by it.

John-Roger and Peter McWilliams add: "You don't have to *like* your parents. But it can help heal you if you learn to love them."

# Three

# FRIENDS

*Friendship is constant in all other things /
Save in the office and affairs of love.*

—*Much Ado About Nothing*

Sometimes the categories of friends and family overlap. Sometimes they are related by contrast. Hugh Kingsmill viewed the first category as compensation for the second: "Friends are God's apology for relations." The seventeenth-century writer and physician Sir Thomas Browne anticipated this sentiment when he confessed in *Religio Medici* that he felt more allegiance to his friends than to his family: "I hope I do not break the fifth commandment [honor thy father and thy mother] if I conceive I may love my friend before the nearest of my blood."

Friendship is a recurrent theme in literature from the ancient world to contemporary writing. "Of all the things that wisdom provides to help one live one's entire life in happiness, the greatest by far is friendship" says Epicurus (c.341–271 B.C.E.). "I count myself in nothing else so happy / As in a soul rememb'ring my good friends," says Bolingbroke in Shakespeare's *Richard II*

(2.3.46–47). In the twenty-first century, friends are the new family: look at the New York sofa sixsome of TV's *Friends*. Friends are family that one has chosen.

I was on holiday one year with a girlfriend when I ran out of reading material on the flight home; she ripped her paperback in half so I could share it. Now that's friendship! When this same friend and I got our first jobs (in different professional spheres, in different parts of the globe) we equipped our wardrobe with some very expensive suits that we shared. Now that's friendship! I have always loved the sisterhood of friendship, the long confessional conversations, the parallel paths and different discoveries, the sharing of advice and experience and sympathy (and clothes).

Friendships today, particularly female friendships, often function like romantic relationships; they are intimate and intense. Consequently they are subject to the same pressures as romantic relationships. If friends do not move up the career ladder in sync, one of them can feel undermined or resentful. Relocation to other cities causes stress. Loyalties—to job or friend, to lover or friend—are tested. Today's mobile and impermanent world can lead to insecurities that friendships register quickly. It is notable that women tend to use the same strong vocabulary for friendships as they do for romantic relationships: betrayal, rejection, neglect, love, loyalty, devotion.

Many of my friends live in other cities and countries. I am not good at regular communication—and neither are they!—but we always pick up without a time lag. However, I have colleagues whose female friends are high maintenance, making demands on time and emotion akin to those of a lover. One of them needs to appease her friend with daily phone calls and regular meetings, and is reproached if she lapses in attention. Another must always be available on her friend's birthday. Another ran into her possessive girlfriend when she was taking a visiting colleague out to lunch; the sidewalk hellos were cold and suspicious, and my colleague felt as if she had been caught in flagrante delicto.

"Strangers are just friends you don't yet know" says a twentieth-century cliché. Victoria Coren offers a satirical update of this last comment: "Strangers are just friends you don't yet fear, resent and compete with." Underneath this comic cynicism is a serious question, however, one often posed by Shakespeare: what happens to friendship when it comes under pressure? Modern writers have attempted to answer this question. Here is Oscar Wilde: "Anybody can sympathize with the sufferings of a friend but it requires a very fine nature . . . to sympathize with a friend's success." And Gore Vidal confessed: "Whenever a friend succeeds, a little something in me dies."

In the last chapter we looked at the effect of marriage on family relationships. Here I want to look at the pressure marriage puts on friendship. An old proverb says, "A friend married is a friend lost." Shakespeare is alert to this potential conflict.

Marriage is threatening to friendship for the same reason it is threatening in family life: it destabilizes the status quo. When Antonio, the merchant of Venice, writes to his newly married friend Bassanio asking to see him before he dies, he concludes his request with a barbed conditional: "if your love do not persuade you to come, let not my letter" (3.2.321–22). The request subtly (or rather, not so subtly) tests his friend's allegiance: is it to his new wife or to his old friend? Because the play is a comedy, the new wife supports the allegiance to the old friend, so the tension is diffused (temporarily at least). But marriage changes the situation in friendship so profoundly that it is generally easier if friends embark on marriage at the same time. "Get thee a wife, get thee a wife" is newly wed Benedick's not entirely disinterested advice to his friend Don Pedro in *Much Ado About Nothing* (5.4.122). Bassanio might offer the same advice to Antonio as a remedy for the inexplicable sadness with which he begins (and presumably also ends) the play. At least, the sadness is inexplicable to Antonio ("In sooth, I know not why I am so sad"; 1.1.1), but it is easily explained in terms of human psychology if we remember that he is about to lose his friend to wedlock.

Falling in love at the same time as a friend is thus a good idea. However, fancying your best friend's partner isn't. "Then will two at once woo one," exclaims Puck in anticipatory glee in *A Midsummer Night's Dream* when he realizes that his error with the magic love juice compels two men to love the same woman. "That must needs be sport alone" (3.2.118–19). But the situation is never funny, even in *A Midsummer Night's Dream*. In this play Helena, the object of two men's simultaneous affection, assumes that their extravagant competition in courtship is simply part of a conspiracy to humiliate her. Instead of accepting one man, she rejects both (at least, until Puck reverses his mistake with the love juice).

In one of Shakespeare's earliest plays, *The Two Gentlemen of Verona*, Proteus meets Silvia, the beloved of his best friend, Valentine, only to find himself instantly in love with her. Proteus's love for Silvia quickly overturns his friendship and loyalty to Valentine (to say nothing of his earlier vows to his own beloved, Julia). Proteus is aware that he is doubly forsworn but tries to justify his treachery with some fancy rhetorical footwork: "If I keep them [both friend and girlfriend], I needs must lose myself " (2.6.20). Implicitly acknowledging that friendship is the highest good, he argues that he is still showing friendship—to himself! ("I to myself am dearer than a friend"; 2.6.23).

Proteus tells Silvia's father of Valentine's plan to elope with Silvia; Valentine is consequently banished; Silvia flees to the forest to look for him; and Proteus follows Silvia to the forest. Silvia reminds Proteus of his friendship to Valentine but Proteus dismisses this consideration with a glib rhetorical question: "In love / Who respects friend?" (5.4.53–54). Unable to get Silvia to accept his love suit (she remains true to Valentine), Proteus resorts to rape: "if the gentle spirit of moving words / Can no way change you to a milder form, . . . / I'll force thee yield to my desire" (5.4.55–56, 59). At this point, as one critic observes, there are *no* gentlemen in Verona.

Valentine fortunately arrives on the scene in time to prevent the rape, at which point Proteus's shame and contrition become as extreme as his earlier disloyalty. Valentine accepts his friend's apologies and, to show there are no hard feelings, offers to give up Silvia to Proteus! The men discuss who should have her, all the while paying no attention to Silvia. Friendship is now more important than love, and Silvia is reduced to a pass-the-parcel exchange.

The play belongs to a period when male friendship was one of the highest forms of love. But the play places the love/friendship opposition in the context of a larger debate about human loyalty. "Were man / But constant, he were perfect," moralizes Proteus in the last act (5.4.110–11). Proteus's treachery to his friend, Valentine, and Valentine's willingness to sacrifice his love, Silvia, to his friend are different but equally reprehensible displays of inconstancy.

Launce, the clown, shows us how shallow the behavior of these young men is. Launce has a dog called Crab, and he tells a story of an occasion on which Crab got loose in Silvia's family dining room, stole the dinner meat, urinated under the table and then again on exit, this time against Silvia's skirt. To save his dog from whipping, Launce takes Crab's transgression upon himself, saying that it was he, Launce, who urinated! Launce is therefore whipped instead of his dog. This is not the first time that Launce has intervened on behalf of his pet: "I have sat in the stocks for puddings he hath stol'n, otherwise he had been executed; I have stood on the pillary for geese he hath kill'd, otherwise he had suffer'd for't" (4.4.30–33). Launce's unwavering loyalty contrasts with the activities of the two gentlemen of Verona. Now that's friendship.

For the Elizabethans male-male friendship defined a man as masculine. Real men, it seems, don't have sex. To us today heterosexual love is the indicator of a "real man," but in Shakespeare's time to love a woman was to risk being branded as effeminate. "O sweet Juliet, / Thy beauty hath made me effeminate, / And in my temper soft'ned valor's steel" wails Romeo (3.1.113–15). He means simply that love has made him a pacifist, that he has lost his masculine martial alacrity, his fighting spirit. But there is something oddly detumescent in his image of soft steel. For us, Romeo's perceived predicament is a contradiction— if you are having sex with a woman, you cannot be a softie—but in the 1590s to be a man was to love another man.

By this I do not mean homosexuality or sodomy or any of the other inadequate and judgmental terms that bear no relation to Elizabethan cultural practice and attitude. By loving a man I mean having allegiance to a male over a female. In *Coriolanus* the soldiers Tullus Aufidius and Coriolanus bond in mutual martial admiration to such an extent that their relationship is elevated above marriage. Tullus Aufidius tells Coriolanus that seeing him "more dances [makes dance] my rapt heart / Than when I first my wedded mistress saw / Bestride my threshold" (4.5.116–18).

In *The Two Noble Kinsmen* Palamon and Arcite swear undying

friendship in a dialogue that also borrows marital images: "We are one another's wife" (3.2.80). When Palamon opines that their friendship will never end, Arcite responds in terms which echo the wedding service: "Till our deaths it cannot" (2.1.173–74). When both men subsequently fall in love with the same woman, the friendship is severed first by enmity and then by death. As Claudio says in *Much Ado About Nothing*, "Friendship is constant in all other things / Save in the office and affairs of love" (2.1.175–76). Friends become friends because they like the same things; but paradoxically, if they like the same thing—the same woman—they cease to be friends. Love turns friends into betrayers, competitors, foes.

Shakespearean women have friendships too. In *A Midsummer Night's Dream* Helena lyrically reminds Hermia of a shared childhood in which the two functioned as one: they sewed one flower on one sampler together, sitting on one cushion, singing one song, in one key, "so we grew together, / Like to a double cherry, seeming parted, / But yet an union in partition" (3.2.209–10). Helena chastises Hermia for her apparent willingness to risk this shared heritage (Puck's mistake means that Hermia's boyfriend now woos Helena, and Helena assumes Hermia is part of a plot to scorn her): "And will you rent our ancient love asunder, / To join with men in scorning your poor friend? / It is not friendly, 'tis not maidenly" (3.2.215–17). Does this last line comprise two separate observations—that is, Hermia's behavior violates both friendship and womanhood? Or is the second observation in apposition to the first, with "maidenly" (feminine, virginal) being a synonym for "friendly"? *The Two Noble Kinsmen* supports the latter interpretation. In this play Emilia reminisces at length about her childhood friendship with Flavina (now deceased), concluding that the "true love 'tween maid and maid" exceeds heterosexual love (she says it is "more than in sex dividual"; 1.3.81–82). If this is the case for both men and women—that same-sex love exceeds heterosexual love—then heterosexual marriage does not seem an emotionally satisfactory resolution unless same-sex attachment is simply a formative phase that has to be left behind as one enters adulthood.

Shakespeare's women often appear as part of a female pair. There are cousins: Rosalind and Celia in *As You Like It*, Beatrice and Hero in *Much Ado About Nothing*. Sisters: Katherine and Bianca in *The Taming of the Shrew*, Adriana and Luciana in *The Comedy of Errors*, Emilia and Hippolyta in *The Two Noble Kinsmen*. Friends: Hermia and Helena in *A Midsummer Night's Dream*, Mrs. Page and Mrs. Ford in *The Merry Wives of Windsor*. Mistress and servant: Portia and Nerissa in *The Merchant of Venice*, Desdemona and Emilia in *Othello*. In almost all cases the two act as each other's confidante, sharing hopes and feelings. Where they do not—as in the case of Katherine and Bianca—the separation is part of the play's thematic point: Katherine and Bianca represent different types of womanhood, one independent and trying to be herself, one apparently conventional. They have different value systems; they can have nothing to say to each other, literally.

If young men and women have friends, so too do politicians. The dying Henry IV tells his son, the future Henry V, that "my friends, which thou must make thy friends, / Have but their stings and teeth newly ta'en out" (*2 Henry IV* 4.5.204–5). Political friends are those who may sting and bite, and so have to receive preventive surgery; as one critic says, this is a very depressing picture of what friendship means in politics. It is even more depressing when we consider that Henry IV was once the Bolingbroke who, as we saw at the opening of this chapter, counted himself in nothing else so happy as in a soul remembering his good friends. Has "friend" in this context now come to mean no more than "voter"? In the same play the country justice Shallow decides to cultivate Falstaff because "a friend i'th'court is better than a penny in purse" (*2 Henry IV* 5.1.30–31). In the world of Shakespearean politics friends are not humans but financial investments.

What is yet more depressing is that Bolingbroke's observation about political friends being animals with teeth has not changed in four hundred years. At the end of the twentieth century the British politician Alan Clark offered an eerie echo of Bolingbroke when he said, "There are no true friends in politics. We are all sharks circling, and waiting for traces of blood to appear in the water."

As a child I had an imaginary friend called Janice. She was a fixture of my childhood from an early age, as real to me as my other friends at kindergarten and primary school. A neighbor was disconcerted one day when she met me seeking a lost Janice and helped me in my search. My mother arrived on the scene to explain that Janice wasn't really missing because she wasn't actually real. But despite her lack of corporeality Janice accompanied me on vacation, sat beside me at meals, and listened to my monologues. This continued until I was about seven; by then I had outgrown Janice, so she was retired.

More than 50 percent of children have imaginary friends. These fictitious playmates help children in important ways: they allow children to be in control at a time when everyone in their life is in control of them (I was forever reprimanding Janice, exhorting her, telling her how to behave). They allow children to test emotions and situations (such as fear or anger) or social challenges (such as starting school) in situations of safety (Janice was afraid of the dark and did not like meeting strangers). They allow children to try out different ways of seeing things: a "good" child may have a "naughty" friend and vice versa. In this last respect, the imaginary friend is the childhood equivalent of a Shakespeare play: a creative work, a work of the imagination, that enables the friend/reader to experience different ways of viewing the world. "See better." Children with imaginary friends are better at seeing things from another's perspective, at understanding authority, concepts of right and wrong, discipline. Emotionally and cognitively an imaginary friend helps the child understand identity: others' and his/her own. The abstract nature of a friend helps the child process abstractions—emotions—in relation to him- or herself and work out who he or she is.

My childhood friendships with boys (real, not fictitious) were less harmonious. To earn admittance to the circle of eight-year-old males, my sister and I had to pass a test: running barefoot along a railway embankment of nettles. We did as required but were never convinced that the reward of male friendship was worth the pain involved in earning it.

Ideologically, of course, this is an unviable situation: friendship is offered, not earned; it is involuntary, not subscribed. When two people are friends, they simply cannot help it. This is the situation described by the Renaissance essayist Michel de Montaigne, in his essay "On Friendship" when he describes his feelings for his friend La Boétie:

> If I were pressed to say why I love him, I feel that my only reply could be: "Because it was he, because it was I." There is, beyond all my reasoning, and beyond all that I can specifically say, some inexplicable power of destiny that brought about our union.

This is the language we associate today with romantic love: an external power, an unexplained attraction, feelings that cannot be expressed except by acknowledging that two individuals are one: "it was he, . . . it was I." This is the matrimonial language that we saw Shakespeare's male characters using to describe friendship in *Coriolanus* and *The Two Noble Kinsmen*.

It is also, as critic Richard Scholar points out, the language of Shakespeare's women when they describe love. In *A Midsummer Night's Dream* (1.1.59) Hermia says, "I know not by what power I am made bold." (But we do: the power is love). In *Much Ado About Nothing* Beatrice and Benedick confess their love for each other with the same formula. "I do love nothing in the world so well as you," says Benedick; "—is not that strange?" "As strange as the thing I know not," responds Beatrice (4.1.269). When you encounter the thing you know not, writes Scholar, you encounter love.

Or hate. The dividing line between love and hate, between friends and enemies, is slim. Enmity is our emotional protection against similarity: often what we dislike in our foes is that they remind us of ourselves. In an essay on *The Merchant of Venice* Richard Scholar points out that "no two characters in the play are more similar than Shylock and Antonio." Both are motivated by hatred; this mutual hatred binds them as much as it divides them. Of the friendship of Leontes and Polixenes in *The Winter's Tale*—a friendship that goes back to childhood—Professor Stephen Orgel observes, "friendship is hospitality but also competition . . . The best friend is also the rival who makes you feel insecure." Sympathy can quickly become antipathy because, as Richard Scholar observes, they were never far apart to begin with.

*Much Ado About Nothing* illustrates this by chronicling *two* reversals in love/friendship: from love to hate to love again. Beatrice and Benedick were lovers before the play opened. By the time we meet them at the start of act 1, they are enemies. They conduct a "merry war of words"—merry for the bystanders, that is, but at times barbed and painful for the participants. Their enmity is a form of community, however, as their friends realize, and by the end of the play the couple agree to marry. The vocabulary of peace and war, of friend and foe, of lover and enemy, are intertwined throughout.

The alternating enmity and friendship of Beatrice and Benedick in *Much Ado* is part of a larger battle: the battle of the sexes. This battle is in turn related to the question of identity. So far we have looked at the stress placed on identity by society (chapter 1), family (chapter 2), and friendship (chapter 3). Let us now look at the pressure gender stereotypes place on identity and relationships.

# four

# THE BATTLE
# OF THE SEXES:
# COMEDY

*Do you not know I am a woman?*
*when I think, I must speak.*

—*As You Like It*

The battle of the sexes is a term usually associated with comedy. In that context it has a long history: the shrewish wife (Noah's wife in medieval drama, Chaucer's Wife of Bath, Shakespeare's Katherine in *The Taming of the Shrew*); the evenly matched sparring partners of *Much Ado About Nothing* (Beatrice and Benedick) or Restoration comedy (Mirabel and Millamant in Congreve's *Way of the World*); the farcical domestic violence of *Punch and Judy* puppet theater; the misogynist jokes of twentieth-century stand-up comedians ("I haven't spoken to my wife for over a month," says Les Dawson. "We haven't had a row—it's just that I'm afraid to interrupt her."). All the above examples center on the stereotype of the talkative wife.

On the Renaissance stage female speech was socially

unorthodox but theatrically comic; indeed it was comic because it was unorthodox, violating social conventions. Comedy defused the threat. The talkative wife was tamed and corrected; or if she was triumphant, that was the sort of thing that only happened in plays.

Female speech was not approved of in the Renaissance unless the wife spoke at her husband's request and echoed his opinions. Independent speech represented independence of thought, the latter clearly an intellectual impossibility in an age that viewed the wife as the moon to the husband's sun (reflecting his light) and seriously debated whether women had a soul (Genesis mentioned Eve's body as separate but said nothing about her soul).

And if women were allowed to voice independent *thoughts*, there was no telling what other autonomous behavior they might want. Sexual independence, for example: the right to go out unchaperoned, to meet other men, to be unfaithful. Thus, independent female speech came to represent independent female sexuality: a woman who would open one orifice (her mouth) indiscriminately would open another . . . The silent woman was by definition a chaste woman.

What literary tradition calls the "battle of the sexes" today often counts as sexism. In this chapter and the next I want to look at three areas (society at large, the workplace, the home) in which Shakespearean women encounter sexism in their journey to be themselves.

*All's Well That Ends Well* is Shakespeare's version of *Men Are from Mars, Women Are from Venus*. John Gray's perceptive analysis of the difference in communication styles between men and women has been deservedly influential. In Gray's work the Mars-Venus opposition is a metaphor to indicate that the two sexes come from different planets and have different verbal and emotional characteristics. In Shakespeare the Mars-Venus opposition is applied more literally. *All's Well That Ends Well* investigates the difficulties encountered by its heroine, Helen, in trying to be herself in an era when men are characterized by Mars (the god of war) and women by Venus (the god of love).

Helen is in love with Bertram, whose father has just died. Bertram is sent to the French court in Paris, to grow up under the guardianship of the king. Having left a house of mourning, Bertram is eager to experience the world. The French court is preparing to send its young men to assist in the Italian wars, but Bertram is frustrated when his youth renders him ineligible for military service. He complains that he is kept in Paris, that he is fobbed off with "too young" and "next year" and "'tis too early," and he describes himself as "the forehorse to a smock" (that is, the head of a team of women; 2.1.28, 30). Bertram wants to be with the men; he wants to be a man.

He is further restricted by an arranged marriage. Helen has inherited her dead father's medical skills and medicines, and when she heals the king, he grants Helen her choice of Bertram as husband. This is the last straw for Bertram and he runs away to war. Military activity, under the jurisdiction of Mars, is traditionally where boys become men. Bertram enthusiastically invokes the god of war:

> Great Mars, I put myself into thy file;
> Make me but like my thoughts, and I shall prove
> A lover of thy drum, hater of love. (3.3.9–11)

But war is not the only arena for proving manhood. Sex is also an important rite de passage. Although he is resistant to marriage and is a "hater of love," Bertram is not averse to sex. In

Florence he tries to seduce a young virgin, Diana. His attempted seduction is described in terms of warfare. He "lays down his wanton *siege* before [Diana's] beauty" (3.7.18), but Diana, we are told, "is *arm'd* for him, and keeps her *guard* / In honestest *defense*" (3.5.73–74). For Bertram, sex and battle merge, both under the auspices of Mars. Sex and battle are both arenas in which he can aggressively prove himself a man.

For Elizabethan men, military glory was synonymous with masculine honor. For Elizabethan women, "honor" had a different meaning: virginity. When Bertram refuses Diana's request that he give her his family ring, because it represents his family honor and as such would be "the greatest obloquy in the world in [him] to lose," Diana turns both his logic and his language back on him:

> Mine honor's such a ring,
> My chastity's the jewel of our house . . .
> Which were the greatest obloquy i'th'world
> In me to lose. Thus your own proper wisdom
> Brings in the champion Honour on my part,
> Against your vain assault. (4.2.45–51)

Diana, as befits her namesake, the goddess of chastity, wishes to retain her virgin honor.

Helen, however, has a different attitude. In the play's first scene she engages in a conversation with one of Bertram's followers about how a woman may (1) barricade her virginity against the enemy, man; and, failing that, (2) how a woman may "lose it to her own liking." Elizabethan women were not supposed to have a "liking" for sex. Critics have condemned Helen for her frankness, and for her eagerness to substitute for Diana in the bedroom. (She encourages Diana to agree to Bertram's sexual request, but it is actually Helen who spends the night with Bertram.) Throughout the play Helen pursues Bertram in France, in Italy, at court, and in the bedroom. As a result she is in danger, as she herself realizes, of being charged with "impudence [that is, immodesty], / A strumpet's boldness, a divulged shame" (2.1.170–71). Simply put, a woman who wants sex must be shameless.

Impudence was a stronger word then than now. It has its roots in the Latin *pudens*, ashamed, the same Latin root which gives us the word pudendum, body parts of which to be ashamed. Thus the impudent reputation that Helen realizes may attach to her because of her determined actions in public life is a specifically sexual reputation. Indeed, she uses "a strumpet's boldness" as a synonym for impudence.

Literature, like life, knows how to categorize the modest virgin, and it knows how to categorize her opposite, the whore. What Helen wants is the pleasure of lawful married sex. She has been married to Bertram in a public ceremony but has not yet confirmed the tie sexually. Elizabethan society had no category in which to slot this legitimate female sexual desire. Bertram's journey in the field of Mars is thus easier than Helen's in the field of Venus, for he at least does not encounter a societal double standard. When he ventures from the military field to the sexual, his sexual peccadilloes are viewed as adolescent experiment: "Certain it is I lik'd her," he says of Diana and his supposed tryst, "And boarded her i'th'wanton way of youth" (5.3.210–11). Diana, on the other hand, is viewed as a "common customer" for her putative sexual encounter (5.3.286).

Contemporary events remind us of the prejudices faced by Helen and Diana. The William Kennedy-Smith rape trial in 1991 made much of the fact that the victim wore underwear from Victoria's Secret. In fact underwear often plays a part in the reporting of rape cases. A recent British case noted (with a what-can-you-expect rhetorical frown) that the teenage victim was wearing underpants with a sexually provocative motto.

But Shakespeare's careful choice of female names in the play points out the reductive sexual stereotyping of women in his age. He gives Diana the name of the mythological goddess of chastity and gives Helen the name of the mythological queen whose sexual activity led to the Trojan War. For the Elizabethans there was only one Helen—Helen of Troy (just as for us today there is only one Hitler). And Helen was not just a byword for beauty (as she is today) but a byword for wanton sexuality—a woman who left her husband for sexual pleasure with another man. But between these stereotyped sexual extremes lies a healthy halfway house: female enjoyment of, and desire for, married sex.

In chapter 1 we saw how Shakespeare investigates the struggles of characters to avoid being limited by their names. Diana's experiences in the play confirm her in her name's association with chastity: she is so disillusioned by Bertram's deceitful behavior, which she takes as typical of his countrymen, that she resolves to "live and die a maid" (4.2.74). Helen's experiences, on the other hand, confirm her in her pursuit of active marital love, and she has to persuade society (and later critics) that her behavior is not like that of her sexually notorious namesake.

A similar sexual binary haunted the influential Hollywood film *Fatal Attraction* (1987) in which Glenn Close portrayed a successful single publisher, Alex Forrest, who pursued a married man, Dan Gallagher (played by Michael Douglas). In this case the binary was between predatory professional female and innocent married wife.

Alex was depicted in nonrealistic terms (a publisher whose apartment lacked bookcases!) and in surreal surroundings (living in a meatpacking district where bleeding carcasses reinforced her raw animal physicality). These unrealistic images culminated in two scenes whose imagery was drawn from Renaissance witchcraft. Dan's wife, Beth, returned home one day to find their daughter's pet rabbit simmering in a pot on the stove (the scene only lacked a cauldron to make its point); and at the end of the film when Beth, in self-defense, tried to drown Alex in the bathtub, the long immersion led not to Alex's death but to her unexpected revival. (The Elizabethan do-it-yourself witch-detective kit involved immersing the suspect in a pond or river. If she drowned, she was innocent; if she didn't, she wasn't . . . ) Thus the film's imagery presented Alex as deviant: a witch.

Throughout, the film relied on the contrast of sexual stereotypes. Alex's provocative underwear contrasted with Beth's white cotton. Whereas late-night marital sex was prevented or interrupted by the couple's daughter climbing into their bed or the dog needing to be walked, nothing got in the way of adulterous sex. In one thematically important scene, Dan and Alex had sex with Alex sitting in her kitchen sink. This, the film suggested, was how to unite passion and domesticity; yes, you can have both extremes. (Here was the 1980s version of Helen's attempt in *All's Well* to unite stereotyped extremes.)

Despite this moment, the film never approved of Alex. I am not protesting about its condemnation of the home wrecker—given the portrayal of Beth it was impossible not to side with the happily married couple whose life was threatened by an obsessive stalker. But I do feel strongly about the film's stereotyping of female opposites—the sweet domestic wife versus the dangerous, destructive career woman. This film set back the position of professional women by decades. The condemnatory view of Alex as predator transferred to Glenn Close herself, whose determination to win the film role was portrayed as unhealthily obsessive, like that of her character.

Helen's determination to get what she wants in *All's Well*, like Glenn Close's determination to get the role of Alex, is made difficult by the expectations society has of acceptable female behavior. How can Helen be herself—resourceful, determined—when society tells her that these traits are not feminine?

Shakespeare does not answer this question, but he chronicles the struggle and applauds Helen's attempt to be what she wants to be, and to do what she wants to do, against the prevailing norm. For Shakespeare the categories of male and female are simply a larger form of the problem we examined in chapter 1: the problem of the label. Male and female are labels that can interfere with one's sense of self.

In a comedy he wrote a few years before *All's Well*, Shakespeare shows the central characters negotiating gender roles positively. *As You Like It* offers a cross-dressed heroine, Rosalind. Rosalind not only disguises herself as a man, she explores what it is to be masculine. Rosalind tries out the masculine side of her personality, initiating conversations, negotiating finances, brokering marriages. She had originally donned this disguise for practical reasons: to safeguard herself against robbers during her flight from the court to the Forest of Arden where she hoped to meet up with her exiled father. But she retains this disguise long after it has served its protective purpose. Early in the play she tells us that she has met her father and had a conversation with him; but she does not reveal her identity to him—as a woman or his daughter—because she is clearly enjoying her masculine freedom too much to part with it.

The hero, Orlando, does not change costume but he too changes his gendered behavior: in looking after his aged weak servant, Adam, he adopts a protective maternal role (the text explicitly characterizes Orlando in feminine terms as a "doe" looking after his "fawn"; 2.7.128). In his forest meetings with Rosalind he becomes the passive partner, receiving instructions.

Given societal expectations in 1599, these role reversals cannot be permanent. Neither can the holiday freedom of the forest. (In fact, it is the forest location—free from the constraints of convention—that enables Rosalind and Orlando to behave in ways unsanctioned by society.) At the end of the play identities are revealed, marriages solemnized, and the lovers prepare to return to court. But they return as different people from those they were when they first entered the forest. Having experienced a different part of themselves, they are expanded, integrated personalities. They have become more themselves.

Unfortunately for the later Helen, gender stereotypes are not always as open to negotiation as they are in *As You Like It*. Even today they can seem unhealthily rigid. Men are allegedly linear and project focused whereas women, who use both sides of their brain, are credited with the ability to multitask. In fact, this statement has a factual evolutionary basis: in a hunter-gatherer society the hunter had to be focused and logical whereas the female had to be alert to peripherals (whether plants or people). I recently read an article that offered pertinent advice about how women can learn from gender differences. The advice and situations were familiar to us from Shakespeare.

Men focus on outcomes, solutions, the immediate goal. Women tend to think about knock-on effects: if I say this, he might feel hurt; if I do that, he might misinterpret it. A study of five-year-olds in the schoolyard found that girls resisted group leadership because they did not want to appear bossy. This antic-ipation of others' reactions (which, in most other situations, would be a skill and an enviable sensitivity) leads women to be indirect about what they really want. Even Cleopatra, a confi-dent, mature world leader, can't bring herself to tell the depart-ing Antony what she wants from him, skirting round the subject with a series of false starts: "Sir, you and I must part, but that's not it; / Sir, you and I have lov'd, but there's not it; / Something it is I would—" (1.3.86–88). Men just get to the point. The ad-vice? In romantic or work relationships, state what you want. Rather than being upset, your partner will be relieved he doesn't have to read your mind.

Women tend to apologize when delegating tasks or asking favors, even when they deserve them (a pay raise, for instance; help with the shopping). They talk like they don't believe in their own worth, using words like "I feel" and "maybe." In *All's Well That Ends Well* Helen asks her husband a favor but prefaces it with a statement saying that she doesn't deserve it (or him): "I am not worthy of the wealth [that is, her husband] I owe" (2.5.79). The advice? Begin your sentences confidently with "I think," "I believe."

To offer advice about what women can learn from men may imply that the traffic is one way: that women must adopt male attitudes and that men have nothing to learn from women. This is not the case. In business circles, female attributes are becom-ing part of management speak. "Emotional management" and "empathetic leadership" are sought-after qualities. In home life, "new" men with equal responsibility for child care acknowledge that they have gained pleasures denied their own fathers.

"Why can't a woman be more like a man?" asks Professor Higgins in Shaw's *Pygmalion*. His pupil, Eliza, might have posed the question in reverse: "Why can't a man be more like a woman?" Shakespeare answers both questions: they can. And they should. Liberation from gender restrictions enhances our understanding of ourselves. Rosalind does not become "masculine" after her experiment with male autonomy in *As You Like It;* she becomes more herself. And Orlando does not become "feminine"; he becomes an expanded Orlando.

A few years ago I saw an intriguing advertisement in the cinema. A young male office worker was busy at the photocopying machine when a friendly golden retriever bounded in to the room. The dog wagged its tail; the man patted the dog. Over the next minute or more, the dog's behavior moved from the flatteringly affectionate to the boisterously intrusive. It rubbed its body against the man's legs, licked his hand, jumped up at his waist, got in his way as he tried to access the machine, caught his tie in its teeth, and eventually prevented the man from carrying out his task of photocopying. The man's initial welcoming response to the dog's friendliness changed to irritation as his commands of "down, boy" were ignored and then became alarm at the physical invasion. What was this film sequence advertising? That was the question I was asking too. At the end the following words appeared on screen: "This Is What Sexual Harassment Feels Like."

The word "harassment" comes from the French verb *harer,* which means to set a dog on someone. (Did the makers of the advertisement know this?) In English the verb "harass" means to exhaust someone by repeatedly annoying them, importuning them. It is not to be confused with the verb "harry," which comes from Old English and means to make predatory raids, to assault physically. Having beaten her messenger, Cleopatra repents, "That so I harried him" (3.3.40). The Elizabethans knew the verb "to harry"; they did not yet have the verb "to harass," which only came into use in the seventeenth century.

Nonetheless, the Elizabethans were no strangers to the *concept* of harassment. In *Measure for Measure*, a comedy written the year before *All's Well That Ends Well*, Shakespeare shows how gender stereotypes can leave women vulnerable to inappropriate sexual advances. This is not a chapter about sexual harassment: we do not need a Shakespeare play to tell us that harassment is iniquitous. But in *Measure for Measure* Shakespeare uses a plot about harassment to lead in to the larger issue of the battle of the sexes, and in particular, the problems when the female voice is ignored or overruled.

Angelo, the acting governor of Vienna, has been put in power while the duke is on leave. His brief is specific: to clean up a city whose promiscuity has become a problem after years of laxity. Angelo is the ideal candidate for the job because he has a reputation for being rigid and puritanical. Lucio, one of the gossips in the play, tells us that Angelo is not human (he is the product of a mermaid or two dried codfish) and that when he "makes water his urine is congealed ice" (3.2.110–11). The description is comically exaggerated, the stuff of *National Enquirer* headlines. But there's no smoke without fire and we might suspect from such a description that Angelo's sexual self-discipline is what Freud would later call repression. Certainly, the absent duke suspects that Angelo is not as angelic as his name would lead us to believe. Why else would the duke hang around Vienna in disguise as a friar?

Isabella, a novice nun, hears that her brother, Claudio, has made his fiancée pregnant. Under Angelo's new-broom-sweeps-clean policy Claudio is condemned to death for pre-marital sex. The distinction between marital sex and premarital sex in this case is a fine one, because in Renaissance England betrothal was as legally binding as marriage. It was actually a form of marriage. Thus Claudio is not an irresponsible rake but a legitimate loving husband. Shakespeare stresses this point to show that Angelo has no tolerant flexibility at all in applying the law.

Shakespeare could have provided several good reasons for Angelo's rigidity. Sexually transmitted diseases, for instance. Syphilis was a relatively new disease, brought from the new world, and Shakespeare's London was trying to deal with its consequences. Sweating tubs in barber-surgeons' shops were thought to provide a cure. So too was a dish of stewed prunes. Brothels provided dishes of stewed prunes for anxious clients so that you could experience cause and cure in one visit. (So prevalent was this treatment that a "dish of stewed prunes" became a slang phrase for a prostitute.) But throughout *Measure for Measure* Shakespeare pointedly excludes any realistic explanatory social background because this would make Angelo's attitude and actions too logical. In punishing sexual activity Angelo is motivated not by public health concerns but by principle.

Isabella goes to Angelo to beg for her brother's life. Angelo agrees, on one condition: that Isabella have sex with him.

As a nun, Isabella is not just a virgin but, in the words of one critic, a "*professional* virgin." She cannot compromise her soul to save her brother's life. (Theological diversion: Isabella assumes she would endanger her soul but her theology here is a bit dodgy. No Christian authority would condemn her for sacrificing her virginity to save a life. Many authorities from Augustine onward make this explicit in writing. Sin is of the will, not of the body. Here, perhaps, is a link between Isabella and Angelo—they are both morally extreme. Isabella views God as a traffic warden, handing out parking tickets with no consideration of extenuating circumstances—rather like an Angelo, in fact.)

Horrified at what Angelo wants her to do, Isabella threatens to denounce him. His response is cool and confident: "Who will believe thee, Isabel? . . . my place i'th'state, / Will so your accusation overweigh, / That you shall stifle in your own report" (2.4.154, 156–58).

"Have sex with me."—"I'll tell the world."—"Who will believe you?" How many times has this situation been repeated throughout history?

Because this is (technically) a comedy, Isabella avoids sex with Angelo but still manages to save her brother's life. The friar who is assisting Isabella introduces her to Angelo's jilted fiancée, Mariana. Angelo had dumped Mariana before the play began. Under the friar's direction, Mariana substitutes for Isabella in bed with Angelo, thus preserving Isabella's virginity, Claudio's life, and cementing legally her earlier betrothal to Angelo.

Although Angelo gets what he wants (or thinks he does), Isabella does not manage to save Claudio's life: Angelo inexplicably decides to go ahead with Claudio's execution. It is only the fortuitous death from natural causes of another prisoner—who coincidentally resembles Claudio—that enables Claudio to survive. Directed by the friar, the executioner sends the head of the Claudio look-alike to Angelo. Claudio remains safely concealed.

It is not until the end of the play that Isabella finds out her brother has been saved, because the friar decides to conceal this information. His rationale is arrogantly pious: despair in the present will lead to greater comfort for Isabella in the future when she finds out the truth. (There's a lot of suspect psychology in this play, to say nothing of dodgy ethics.) Even so, Isabella's experience of harassment is not over. This helpful but controlling friar turns out to be the duke of Vienna in disguise. In act 5 he exposes Angelo as a hypocrite, and then proposes marriage to Isabella.

Unlike Angelo's sexual proposition, a marriage proposal cannot count as sexual harassment. But a marriage proposal to a *nun* is a blatant attempt to override this woman's clearly announced desires and plans for herself and her life. (In George Whetstone's *Promos and Cassandra* (1578), which provided Shakespeare with the story for *Measure for Measure*, the heroine is not a nun. Shakespeare's deliberate change thus invites our critical attention.) A nun's costume and profession say "no" to men just as clearly as does a woman's verbal "no," but, like the verbal "no," Isabella's choice goes unheard. At the end of the play Isabella is simply in a variant of her situation at the beginning, being asked by a man to do something she does not want to do.

We don't know what answer Isabella makes to the duke's proposal as the play does not script a response for her. Modern productions increasingly offer us a far from happy ending—resigned acceptance or outright rejection—as Isabella registers the sad truth: authority figures on whom she relies try to take advantage of her. (Sounds familiar?)

This has been the pattern since the start of the play. Isabella's brother explains that "in her youth / There is a prone and speechless dialect, / Such as move men; beside, . . . well she can persuade" (1.2.181–86). Her looks come first; her speech second. When Lucio asks Isabella to plead to Angelo, he advises her to use feminine wiles: "when maidens sue, / Men give like gods; but when they weep and kneel, / All their petitions are as freely theirs / As they themselves would owe them" (1.4.80–83). In other words: talk and you'll be successful; act like a hysterical woman and you'll get anything you want. Both Claudio and Lucio see women as sexual rather than verbal, and their sexuality is to be exploited.

The effect of this exploitation is shown in the gradual silencing of Isabella. Bold and vocal in the early acts, she talks, as befits her identity as a novice nun, in theological terms. Her case to Angelo rests entirely on the New Testament principle of mercy. It is full of theological words and phrases: pardon, remorse, God, pity, merciful heaven, mercy, soul. She enters a legal situation from a spiritual point of view.

By act 5, however, this has changed. When Angelo is condemned to death, Mariana asks Isabella to plead for his life. This is the appropriate moment for a passionate speech on mercy but Isabella chooses to offer a coldly logical defense: Angelo didn't commit a crime (have sex with her), she says, even though he thought he did, so you can't kill him for his thoughts. The theological fervor has gone. Isabella's subsequent silence is just a technicality: her voice is already extinguished.

*Measure for Measure* is not only a play about sexual harassment. The harassment plot is also part of a much bigger topic: the importance of the female voice, the problem of ignoring it ("what part of 'no' don't you understand?"), and the damage when spirited women are silenced.

One might have hoped that in this day and age the female voice presented no threat to society at large or men in particular. Apparently this hope is premature. A few years ago I attended an Open Day at a school in the north of England. I traveled with a young male colleague; together we were making a presentation about studying English at Oxford. We had done this twice before in previous months and had a model, which I had initiated, of sharing and copresenting. On this particular visit I asked the colleague if he wished to start the proceedings. He accepted. However, he not only introduced the topic but developed it, covered all the shared material, then asked for questions. The inclusive "we" that I had carefully and consistently used on previous occasions was replaced by an authoritative "I." I was surprised at his procedure, offered two supplementary points, and the session concluded. The next day we repeated the presentation at a different school in a different city. On this occasion he not only did all the talking but incorporated my supplements of the previous day, leaving me with nothing to add. It was made abundantly clear to the audience that there was one authoritative voice and that voice was male.

I was slightly piqued but tolerably sanguine: professional identity or rivalry was nothing to get worried about, and, as the colleague grew older, became more secure, or got tenure he would feel less need to be in male control mode. But what bothered me belatedly, and continues to bother me, was the unhealthy message my passivity sent to the many sixteen- and seventeen-year-old girls in the audience. A professional couple, one young male, one older female: but the male is verbally in charge, the woman in a silent, supporting role. How very 1950s. How very 1590s. How unbearably sad in the year 2000.

And how irresponsible of me not to overturn this image . . . I am by nature nonconfrontational. I am comfortable in the driving seat, but if someone else desperately wants that position, I am happy to let them have it. If it matters to them, it doesn't matter to me. But in this instance I realized belatedly that something did matter to me, and what mattered was that young women were being sent an old-fashioned message.

My colleague's sexism—which is what it amounts to—was unwitting and careless (I presume). He had a need to be a leader. And society has conditioned him as a man to be this way. But the knock-on effect of this on the teenage audience was disconcerting. Gender stereotypes are harder to overturn when they are osmotic. To this day I am haunted by the incident. I began this book with a chapter on being one's self. This incident brought home to me the importance of this, not for one's own sake, not for the sake of gender, but for the benefit of other people.

For Shakespeare female autonomy is always equated with female speech. For him silencing a woman is a tragedy (quite literally in cases such as that of Desdemona, smothered with a pillow). This chapter has chronicled the battle of the sexes in the comic arenas of *All's Well That Ends Well* and *Measure for Measure*. I want to explore this subject further as it moves from problem comedy to danger. That requires a separate chapter.

# five

# THE BATTLE
# OF THE SEXES:
# TRAGEDY

*It is excellent / To have a giant's strength;*
*but it is tyrannous / To use it like a giant.*

—*Measure for Measure*

This chapter looks at what happens when anger becomes a ma-
nipulative weapon in the battle of the sexes, turning sparring
into control. My interest in this subject is not just academic. It
will be obvious to anyone who reads chapter 8 on anger that the
behavior I describe there treads a narrow line between bad temper and abuse. In an attempt to decide whether the man in question was hot-tempered and I was oversensitive, or whether he
was abusive and I was threatened, I sat in the library and read
books about verbal abuse.

That abuse is confined to physical violence is a common mis-
conception. Psychologists now identify three different kinds of
abuse: physical abuse, sexual abuse, and psychological abuse.
Psychological abuse is sometimes called verbal abuse because it

is achieved and maintained by verbal manipulation and coercion. Although the definition of verbal abuse could apply equally to women—the "shrew," for instance—female "nagging" in patriarchal cultures is not considered abusive because the power relations are unequal. The shrewish wife is not taking advantage of a powerless individual, nor does law or custom support her attempts at control.

The key to distinguishing verbal abuse from normal, healthy anger and argument is its purpose: control of the partner. Normal anger does not seek to control. The verbal abuser seeks to get his own way, to impose his own view of events, to manipulate. The verbal abuser is an emotional terrorist.

Verbal abuse comes in many forms. It can manifest as countering (that is, blatant contradiction), discounting (denial of the victim's reality, as in "you're overreacting," "you're too sensitive"), diverting (changing the topic), blocking ("I'm not responsible for your reactions"), scoring rhetorical points that fail to address the issue, accusing and blaming, judging and criticizing, trivializing, undermining, threatening ("do what I want or I'll leave / be angry / hit you / get a divorce"), name calling, revising history ("I don't remember saying that"; "I don't see the situation that way"), ordering, and—most important—anger. Anger prevents the possibility of mutuality in the relationship because it is based on inequality: accusation and defense.

Verbal abuse is also accompanied by mercurial moods. A charming, loving partner can unpredictably switch to vituperative outburst or hostile silence, a tactic designed to unbalance the partner. Verbal abuse takes place only in private so that the outside world sees the abuser the way he sees himself: as a decent man. Since the object of verbal abuse is to release the abuser's sense of helplessness by asserting control, it is never followed by an apology, for to apologize would be to relinquish power. Verbal abusers are often very intense, being as excessive in romance as in anger, and their intimate relationships normally move very quickly in the opening stages—another tactic to disarm the victim. Although I use the word "tactic," verbal abuse need not be a consciously planned operation. The abuser is simply reacting to his sense of powerlessness by exerting power over another human being.

Verbal abuse is dangerous. It often leads to physical violence: all physical violence is preceded by a pattern of verbal abuse; it breaks the victim's spirit; and it causes somatic illness and depression in the victim. The victim of verbal abuse responds in exactly the same way as does the victim of physical abuse: she becomes passive, acquiescent, willing to abase herself in any way to appease the abusive partner.

It is obvious from the above summary that several Shakespearean characters fit the profile of the abused woman. Tragic situations can take place in comic plays. The paradigmatic example of the abused woman is Katherine in *The Taming of the Shrew*, ostensibly a comedy. The title of the play functions conveniently as plot summary: a woman of spirit has that spirit broken by her suitor, Petruchio. Katherine's transgression? Speech. The noun "shrew" refers simply to a woman who talks too much. Note, by the way, that there is no equivalent noun for an overtalkative man. Male speech is not a crime!

Renaissance culture stereotyped women as talkative (and therefore unmarriageable) or quiet (and therefore desirable). *The Taming of the Shrew* contrasts the vocally uncontrollable Katherine, who repels all suitors, with her quiet, younger sister, who is surrounded by wooers. Petruchio undertakes to tame Katherine and turn her into a model wife. This he does by a calculated process of verbal and physical disorientation. He contradicts ("counters") Katherine, he prevents her from eating and sleeping, and he behaves irrationally and unpredictably—he hits the priest, swears in church, rejects designer clothing that he has ordered, and beats his servants for trivial reasons. Eventually Katherine submits verbally to this contrary man, agreeing that the sun is the moon and the moon the sun: "And be it moon, or sun, or what you please; / And if you please to call it a rush-candle, / Henceforth I vow it shall be so for me" (4.5.13–15).

Flagrant contradiction, fury, and frustration are the ingredients of that subgenre of comedy known as farce. But, as John Mortimer said, farce is simply tragedy played at one thousand revolutions per minute. The plot of *The Taming of the Shrew* moves so fast that we have no time to think about it. But in real life, violence is tragic, not comic. In real life, repeated angry outbursts by a man for the purpose of controlling a woman are far from funny. In real life, it is not funny to deny a human being food and sleep. On the contrary: these are the tactics of brainwashing cults and political torture, the substance of petitions to governments and letters to Amnesty International. In a famous production of the play at the Royal Shakespeare Company in 1987, Fiona Shaw's Katherine was visibly brainwashed; wearing an institutional white nightdress, she delivered her last speech without emotion, as if by rote.

In defense of Petruchio, we may note, as critics frequently do, that he never actually hits Katherine. This restraint is in marked contrast to one of the play's sources, a ballad in which the husband kills the family horse, salts its hide, beats his shrewish wife until her skin bleeds, then wraps her in the salted horsehide and locks her in the basement. She is later released on the condition that she behave submissively. A reformed creature, she behaves quietly, obediently, dutifully—to the amazement of her assembled family who have been invited to dinner to witness the transformation.

However, no husband is a "good guy" just because he behaves less badly than he might. As Professor Frances E. Dolan, editor of *The Taming of the Shrew*, points out, when Petruchio beats his servants and damages the furniture he reminds Katherine that he has power to hurt his subordinates and property—and hence her, for in Renaissance culture a wife was both subordinate and property. Like the furniture and the servants, Katherine is Petruchio's "household stuff" and can be treated the same way.

Contemporary case studies show that if a man hits the drywall or punches the air next to his girlfriend, if he slams his fist into a chair or kicks the furniture, he will eventually transfer his violence to his partner. Farce may be a world without pain but real life is not. Real-life women need to get help and get out. In a recent television interview, author Naomi Wolf offered a memorable piece of advice: "if you're sleeping with a man who routinely puts you down, get out of that bed."

Katherine does not get help, nor does she get out. Sixteenth-century women couldn't. However, in some interpretations and stage presentations of the play Katherine is not at risk. Petruchio's manipulations, contradictions, and imposed deprivations are seen as a game—a loving tease with the positive psychological aim of behavior modification. Changed behavioral patterns will enable Katherine to find her true loving self, receive societal approval, and live happily ever after.

I like this interpretation a lot because it enables me to read and teach the play without feeling abject misery. Deep down, however, I know that such an interpretation actually makes matters worse for it says that a woman can only find herself with the help of a man, or worse, that a man is entitled to overrule a woman's life choices and behavior choices (see also chapter 7, in which Angelo and the duke assume they can override Isabella's choice of convent life).

In the final scene Katherine gives a long speech about the duty owed by women to their husbands. She is applauded by all on stage, including Petruchio. Paradoxically, she has achieved what she always wanted—the right to speak—but it is surely a Pyrrhic victory for her as a woman if her freedom of speech is dependent on conventional patriarchal content and male cues (she is allowed to speak because her husband tells her to). Here, Shakespeare presents the world that Sir Thomas More had presented earlier in *Utopia*—a place where the citizens have freedom of speech but are denied freedom of *thought*. What profits it a woman if she gain a voice but lose her identity?

Part of the intellectual attraction of *The Taming of the Shrew* is that its misogyny is open to debate. In her long, dutiful speech in act 5 Katherine may be playing Petruchio at his own game, ridiculing his desire for control by exaggerating her submissiveness and so showing him that she is far from tamed. (And this may be what he wanted.) She may be completely extinguished, robotically reciting the patriarchal party line. Or she may be totally in love, her hyperbolic testimony a genuine tribute. (When Meryl Streep played the role in New York an interviewer asked her how she reconciled this speech with her feminism. Streep replied, "Katherine is saying she's so in love with this man that she will do anything for him. I don't have a problem with that. Do you?")

As a literary critic I can see many ways of interpreting this plot about wife taming. As a woman, however, I cannot find the subjugation of a wife fit matter for comic treatment. Shakespeare, I think, was dissatisfied too. He avoided farce in future plays, and his next two abused women appear in tragedies.

~

In *Othello* Iago's wife, Emilia, fits the typical profile of the abused wife, just as Iago fits the classic profile of the abuser.

Dr. Susan Forward, the noted therapist and author of *Men Who Hate Women and the Women Who Love Them*, observes that no one who feels good about himself needs to control another human being; and Iago clearly does not feel good about himself. He is envious of his colleague Cassio for the "daily beauty" in his life (5.1.19); he is sexually suspicious of Othello (he believes that Othello has slept with Emilia); and he is a misogynist, belittling women in general and Emilia in particular. His mercurial moods further mark him as a dangerous man.

Emilia's personality is well-nigh effaced in her desire to please and placate her husband. It is not until the final act, when she realizes that Iago is responsible for Desdemona's death, that she finds the courage to speak out. However, as is so often the case in abusive relationships, this newfound knowledge of the nature of her husband, and her threat to leave ("Perchance, Iago, I will ne'er go home"; 5.2.197), endangers her safety: Iago kills her before she can reveal further truths about his character and actions.

One of the most painful demonstrations of abuse comes in a short scene in a play written at the same time as *Othello*: *Troilus and Cressida*. The Trojan Cressida is delivered to the enemy Greek camp in exchange for a Trojan prisoner of war. She is forced to leave her lover, Troilus, and, immediately on arrival in the Greek camp, is "wooed" by her guard, Diomedes. The scene is traditionally viewed as a scene of seduction, with Cressida being blamed by critics for giving Diomedes the love pledge (the souvenir sleeve) that Troilus had given her just twenty-four hours before. In fact, the scene is a textbook example of abuse.

Shakespeare presents Diomedes as a bully, tout court. Diomedes ignores Cressida's evident pain, ambivalence, and reluctance to give him a love token. He uses a simple tactic—anger—thereby making the episode one of male coercion rather than female agreement. Like many women who are not socialized in outlets for aggression, Cressida cannot handle anger, and her instinct is to halt it at all costs. Psychologists tell us that, when faced with anger, the sensitive and the insecure will apologize for things for which they are not to blame, abase themselves, agree, submit, concede, do anything—including relinquishing Troilus's love token—to stop the angry attitude or rhetoric. "Nay but you part in anger," says Cressida to Diomedes, and Troilus, who is eavesdropping, asks rhetorically, "Doth that grieve thee?" (5.2.45). His interpretation could not be more wrong. It does not grieve Cressida; it frightens her.

The dialogue between Diomedes and Cressida repeats one pattern throughout the scene: she makes a request, he breaks off in evident anger, and she capitulates. Diomedes is on the point of exit several times in the scene, but Cressida cannot let him part in anger. Diomedes gets what he wants, even though it is obvious that this is not what Cressida wants. He overrules her. Diomedes' angry threat of exit, his fifth, is more than Cressida can cope with: "You shall not go. One cannot speak a word / But it straight starts you" (5.2.100–101). She accurately identifies his behavioral pattern (that is, "I can't say anything without you reacting with anger and withdrawal"). He ignores her diagnosis cum plea, uttering only a terse and menacing response: "I do not like this fooling" (5.2.101).

In chapter 8, Anger, we will see that Troilus is also an angry manipulator of Cressida. Diomedes is not Cressida's first abusive relationship.

That abuse has a literary Shakespearean precedent is scant consolation to anyone. Real-life victims do not become literary heroines—at least, not until they are dead. But looking at these literary situations can help us. Abuse is a story with only one ending—extinction. Katherine loses her personality, Emilia her life, and Cressida her autonomy. Understanding these stories may enable us to rewrite our own before it is too late.

This chapter, like the one preceding it, has been about opposition and inequality, and the effect these have on personal identity and human relations. I want now to turn to a more specific category of unequal relations: unrequited love.

# Six

〜∞〜

# UNREQUITED LOVE

*I know I love in vain, strive against hope.*

—*All's Well That Ends Well*

It is human nature to want what we can't have. A flatter stomach; a fatter salary. More sleep; less work. But because they are physical and practical, these things are not beyond the realm of possibility. No matter how remote they currently seem, they are potentially attainable. It lies in us to do something about them; they are the stuff of New Year's resolutions.

When what we can't have is a person, the situation is tricky—such as if a loved one dies, if you can't have a baby, if you love someone who is unavailable.

A person can be unavailable for several reasons. They may have moved on to a new relationship, a second spouse. They may be completely and utterly indifferent to you, either emotionally or in sexual orientation. They may be inaccessible (a teacher, an employer, a movie star). They may be already married. (If they are adulterously married, they are available physically but not emotionally.) This chapter is about loving someone who doesn't love back, for whatever reason.

My first experience of therapy was after the breakup of a relationship. In the course of a summer Mr. Romantic became Mr. Unavailable. I had long known the relationship had no future, but this didn't mean my heart wasn't broken. Whether our pain is emotional or physical (and emotional pain *feels* physical; it feels like swallowing broken glass) the reaction is identical: we will do anything to stop the pain *now*. And the quickest way I could see to stop the pain was to get him back. The problem was that he had quickly moved on to a new girlfriend.

I explained this to the therapist. He shrugged his shoulders in a gesture of benign helplessness: "You have my sympathy. There's nothing I can do."

He was right. I was seeking relief, not a cure.

Love is irrational. Loving someone who doesn't return the feeling is even more irrational. This is not real love but infatuation, obsession, addiction. Yes, it is possible to be addicted to a person! And Shakespeare knows all about addictive and obsessive relationships. Look at Helena in *A Midsummer Night's Dream,* who pursues the object of her affection, Demetrius, even though he tells her plainly, "I do not nor I cannot love you," and, "I am sick when I do look on thee" (2.1.201, 212)—no ambiguity here. Look at Helen in *All's Well That Ends Well,* who follows her man across France, Spain, and Italy, even though he has made his rejection clear in a letter. Look at the jailer's daughter in *The Two Noble Kinsmen,* who goes mad because of her love for Prince Arcite.

Shakespeare has a special word for persisting in irrational love: doting. This word comes from a Middle English verb that means to be foolish, to have feeble brains. In *A Midsummer Night's Dream* the fairy queen, Titania, "dotes" on Bottom the weaver when he is wearing an ass's head (her judgment and vision are affected by magic love juice). In *Romeo and Juliet* Romeo "dotes" on the unresponsive Rosaline before he experiences true love with Juliet. When Friar Lawrence, Romeo's spiritual advisor, advises caution about Romeo's new relationship with Juliet, Romeo protests, "Thou chidst me oft for loving Rosaline." The friar corrects him; he chid Romeo, he says, "for *doting*, not for loving" (2.3.81–82; my emphasis). The former is reprehensible, the latter is not. In *A Midsummer Night's Dream* Demetrius pursues Hermia, a woman who neither loves him nor encourages him, and rejects Helena, the woman whom he once loved. When his affections return to Helena he compares his irrational pursuit of Hermia to an "idle  gaud [worthless trinket], / Which in my childhood I did dote upon" (4.1.167–68). Even Antony characterizes his love for Cleopatra as dotage when he feels guilty about neglecting his professional responsibilities. "These strong Egyptian fetters I must break, / Or lose myself in dotage" (1.2.116–17). Dotage and doting thus consistently denote the irrational and the irresponsible.

They also denote the immature: dotage represents Romeo's first infatuation, Demetrius associates it with childhood. In today's usage the term indicates not childhood but *second* childhood: senility. (The garrulousness associated with old age led Benjamin Disraeli to coin the term "anecdotage"!). But it originates as a term meaning childish vision, something one will outgrow. Dating is good; doting is not.

In the medieval and Renaissance periods there was a special name for the situation in which men were obsessed with women who didn't return the feeling: courtly love. When we first meet Romeo in *Romeo and Juliet* he is in the pose of the typical courtly lover, pining for Rosaline. We never meet Rosaline in the play, but we know a lot about her. She is pale skinned, dark eyed, hard hearted, and related to the Capulets. Given that the Capulets are the mortal enemies of Romeo's family, the Montagues, it is surprising that Romeo does not experience the same romantic and personal vulnerability that he later feels when he falls in love with another Capulet—Juliet. ("Is she a Capulet? / O dear account! My life is my foe's debt" is his reaction when Juliet's nurse tells Romeo the name of the girl he has just danced with; 1.5.117–18.) But courtly love is never destined for marriage, even when the object of adoration is, like Rosaline, single and available. Thus marriage never crosses Romeo's mind in relation to Rosaline. In fact, the courtly love situation was often set up in such a way that the woman did not encourage *because* she was unavailable (that is, married). The point was simply to drive the unsatisfied lover to poetry. (A recent rhyme asks: "Think you, if Laura had been Petrarch's wife / He would have written sonnets all his life?")

The play's first description of Romeo presents him mockingly: an insomniac who spends his time in tearful solitude. When we first meet Romeo he speaks as we would expect, in heady paradoxes, in extravagant hyperboles and similes, in sad sighs. And, it must be said, in conventionally clichéd (and often downright bad) poetry. His youthful infatuation is not taken seriously.

Despite the comic hyperbole, there is no doubt that Romeo suffers from his (non)relationship with Rosaline. Mercutio observes that Rosaline "torments him so, that he will sure run mad" (2.4.5). Benvolio's strategy to ease Romeo's pain is comparative shopping. They will gate-crash the Capulet ball so that Romeo can meet other beautiful women: "Compare her [Rosaline's] face with some that I shall show / And I will make thee think thy swan a crow" (1.2.86–87). As a tactic it has something to recommend it—as Shakespeare says elsewhere, "one fire drives out one fire; one nail, one nail" (*Coriolanus* 4.7.54)—but it is most successful in love when it happens accidentally, rather than when it is made to happen. Finding a new partner just to assuage the pain of the old rarely works in the long term. This is relief, not cure. This is dependence, not love. The partner must be sought for herself, not for her function. You have to fall out of love first; then you can fall in love again.

If courtly love refers to the situation in which a man loves a woman who does not reciprocate his emotion, there is no equivalent term for the parallel situation in which a woman suffers unrequited love. (Therapist Susan Forward's analysis of the situation in modern life simply calls it "loving the man who doesn't love back".) To describe this phenomenon, critics resort not to technical literary terms but to pejorative psychological descriptions. For instance, the obsession of Helen with Bertram in *All's Well* mostly meets with disapproval. The following comment is typical: Helen succeeds in love with a tenacity "too nearly predatory to be completely attractive or satisfying." (Is it the fact that Helen *succeeds* in catching Bertram that critics dislike?)

But the phenomenon is the same, irrespective of gender: the doting man or woman suffers, is in the helpless grip of an obsession that drives them to extremes, that dominates every moment. In *All's Well* Helen explains, "My imagination / Carries no favor [face] in't but Bertram's." She can't imagine life without him: "I am undone, there is no living, none, / If Bertram be away" (1.1.82–85). But he does move away, from the south of France to Paris, and Helen expresses her predicament with an image from idolatry: "now he's gone, and my idolatrous fancy / Must sanctify his reliques" (1.1.97–98). We couldn't find a stronger image for doting: Helen worships an image she has made. ("Fancy" in Shakespeare has the force of imagination as well as "whim.")

$\sim$

Helen may worship Bertram, but he barely registers her existence. Indifference! That is worse than dislike or hatred, for these last two are at least a form of passion. In the first scene

Bertram is preparing to go to the French court in Paris where, as an underage count (his father has just died), Bertram will live as a ward of court. Helen quickly finds an excuse to follow Bertram to Paris where she uses her medical knowledge and spiritual powers to heal the king. In gratitude, the king grants Helen her choice of husband—Bertram. Bertram is (understandably) appalled: "I cannot love her, nor will strive to do't" (2.3.145). Shakespearean heroes don't mince words.

One has some sympathy with Bertram here. When he beseeches the king, "In such a business, give me leave to use / The help of mine own eyes" (2.3.107–8), he demands no more than any Shakespearean heroine demands when surprised by an arranged marriage. Hermia in *A Midsummer Night's Dream* similarly requests that her father look "but with my eyes" (1.1.56). Furthermore, if we approach the situation from Bertram's point of view (ah, yes, that tactic again), we see a young man who has just left home (a *very* young man: remember he is underage), who has just escaped from a house of mourning, who has just left a house of women, and is keen to make his way in the masculine world. He is now surrounded by men; he wants to accompany them to the Italian wars. He is not ready to be a husband. Sometimes the problem with the person who doesn't love back is simply timing. I was still obsessed with Mr. Unavailable because I needed him as a nail to drive out the heartbreak. He needed a nail too but he had found his elsewhere.

Forced by the king into marriage, Bertram behaves coldly to Helen, denies her a kiss, and cannot even bring himself to name her (he refers to her repeatedly as "she"). He sneaks away in the night, leaving Helen a note:

When thou canst get the ring upon my finger, which never shall come off, and show me a child begotten of thy body that

I am father to, then call me husband; but in such a "then" I
write a "never." (3.2.57–60)

This is not just a "don't call me, I'll call you" letter. This is the
Renaissance equivalent of "when hell freezes over."

Most women would be daunted and deterred by such blatant
rejection. Not Helen. She interprets his rejection as a challenge. With marvelous ingenuity and determination, she tricks
Bertram into having sex with her, gets his ring, and becomes
pregnant, thereby fulfilling the conditions of his letter. All's well
that ends well? Not quite. In the final scene Bertram lies, and
tries to wriggle out of the situation, before being forced by over-
whelming evidence to acquiesce. Bertram is as young and shallow and cowardly as he was at the beginning. He and Helen, I
imagine, live unhappily ever after.

That Helen succeeds in gaining her love object is undeniable.
But what does gain mean in this context? She gets her man
physically, not emotionally. As act 5 stands, there's not much
hope for Bertram and Helen's long-term marital happiness.

Helen not only loves a man who doesn't love back; she *persists* in
loving him. She herself is aware that this is hopeless:

I know I love in vain, strive against hope;
Yet in this captious [receptive] and intenible [unretentive] sieve
I still pour in the waters of my love
And lack not to lose still. (1.3.201–4)

(This last line can mean either "I know I'm going to carry on losing" or "I've got enough love to continue pouring away" [lose still].)
A giant sieve provides a pretty clear image of unreciprocated love.

In today's more scientific terminology we would say she is pouring her energy into a black hole. But why?

Robin Norwood's perceptive book about unhealthy relationships, *Women Who Love Too Much*, explains. Loving someone who doesn't love back becomes an addiction, an obsession. And being addicted to a person fills the same emotional voids as addiction to substances (nicotine, alcohol, chocolate) or activities (shopping, Internet surfing, exercise, housework). The unresponsive person provides a focal point for your life ("My imagination / Carries no favor in't but Bertram's") and a raison d'être ("there is no living, none, / If Bertram be away"). Loving the other person becomes a substitute for loving oneself.

There is no doubt that Helen undervalues herself. Her sense of inferiority is cemented in sixteenth-century class issues. As a doctor's daughter—that is, as the daughter of a tradesman—she is scorned: "a poor physician's daughter!" exclaims Bertram in horror. (Odd to think of a world in which the medical profession had no respect.) But although this is the reality in Shakespeare's England, *no one in the play* considers Helen's class a barrier to marrying Bertram. Bertram's mother, the countess of Rossillion, and the king of France both approve of the marriage and encourage it. The king says that Helen lacks only external worth (a title), which he will supply; she herself is virtuous, good, honorable, a "jewel," worthy of Bertram.

But Helen doesn't *feel* worthy. She frequently mentions her sense of inferiority. Her words could be those of any woman today who lacks self-esteem. "Nor would I have him till I do deserve him" she says in act 1 (1.3.199). Despite the finite time scheme implied in the conjunction "till," she cannot imagine a world in which she might deserve Bertram: her next line is "Yet never know how that desert should be" (1.3.200). When the king gives Bertram to her, she draws a distinction, not wanting to be presumptuous: she will not "take" Bertram; she will "give" herself. And when she bids Bertram farewell she tells him "I am not worthy of the wealth I owe" [In Shakespeare's day "owe" meant both own and owe]: (2.5.79). We need no longer be surprised by the plot, by Helen's willingness to lose herself in the relationship, to go to extremes for Bertram's sake. She is trying to "earn" him by "passing a test." No obstacle that Bertram throws in her way is too much for Helen. He leaves the south of France for Paris; she finds an excuse to follow him to court. He runs away to the Italian wars; she travels alone from Paris to Florence. He presents three impossible tasks in his letter of rejection; she fulfills them all. Chapter 3 of *Women Who Love Too Much* is titled, "If I suffer for you, will you love me?" This title describes Helen's behavioral pattern exactly, the behavioral pattern of women who do not value themselves.

The answer to Norwood's rhetorical question is, of course: no, he won't love you if you suffer for him. Your suffering is not evidence of love; it is evidence of need. You cannot love him if you need him this badly—you can only use him, use him to fill the gap in your life, in your heart. You can only use him to stop the pain.

And when we suffer we seek relief, not cure. A cure might provide permanent relief but it involves interim pain, the pain of detaching from the cause of the pain. Easier in the short term to opt for the palliative.

To break the addiction you need to love yourself. And loving yourself is a long-term project; it doesn't happen overnight or in act 5. Robin Norwood (in *Women Who Love Too Much* ) and Howard Halpern (in *How to Break Your Addiction to a Person* ) give strategies for helping the Helens of the world detach and recover from their Bertrams. These strategies include prioritizing the self, spiritually and physically (spiritual need not mean full-blown faith: it can be as simple as a walk in the park, communing with nature); getting external support from friends and professionals (peer support is crucial because it enables you to practice receiving rather than giving, and professional support helps you get where you are going more quickly!); and learning to identify the shortcomings and patterns that got you hooked in the first place (becoming aware of a situation is the first step to being in control of it).

You also need to fall out of love with Mr. Unavailable. Literature tells us a lot about falling in love; it doesn't tell us how to fall out of love. For that we need to turn to one of my favorite contemporary poets, Wendy Cope.

> *Two Cures for Love*
> 1. Don't see him. Don't phone or write a letter.
> 2. The easy way: get to know him better.

With the clear-eyed emotional perception that characterizes her poetry, Cope here gets at the heart of love: it's about imagination, vision, how you see things. (This is an aspect of love that we will examine in its positive aspects in chapter 10.) In this instance Cope's poetic persona is in love with a vision that doesn't exist. Like Helen she is in love with a vision that she has created: "my idolatrous fancy / Must sanctify his reliques." This is also the situation of Olivia in *Twelfth Night*, who is unable to see that Cesario / Viola is really a woman in disguise. Viola realizes that Olivia "seems to dote" on her (that crucial Shakespearean verb again) and says "Poor lady, she were better love a dream" (2.1.26).

Olivia's "dream"; Helen's "fancy." Disabusing oneself of that vision—learning to "see better," to see things correctly—will enable one to fall out of love.

In *How to Mend Your Broken Heart* Paul McKenna and Hugh Willbourn offer helpful strategies for detaching. Their tactics are exactly the kind Shakespeare endorses in his less specialized vocabulary. For McKenna and Willbourn you need to imagine a new future for yourself, one without the loved one. You need to rearrange the furniture, physical and mental. Physical is easy: reposition furniture, buy a cushion, reframe a picture, delete his number from your mobile's memory. Follow the same procedure for your mental furniture. Reframe your loved one (McKenna and Willbourn advise imagining him in spatial terms, in a frame, a frame that is being moved farther and farther away until it has shrunk to one-tenth of its size). Stop thinking the loved one is the "only one for you": they point out that that is only true when two people think it true. How can you stop this? Recall five positive memories, replay them like a video, then step out of them; drain the picture of color and clarity, reducing the emotional intensity, reclassifying the memory. Do the same with five negative memories, but now turn up the color and intensity until you no longer wish to replay the experience. You are practicing seeing things differently. Eventually what you see will become true.

For Elizabethans the definition of a comedy was a play that ends in marriage. In *All's Well That Ends Well* the marriage occurs in act 2. Marriage is not always a happy ending; sometimes it is an unhappy beginning. (Shakespeare, it seems, knew all about this. He, like Bertram, was trapped into marriage as a teenager but for a different reason: he got his girlfriend, Anne Hathaway, pregnant.) At the end of *All's Well* Bertram is not converted; he is just cornered. Helen gets who she wants; that who she wants doesn't want her seems not to concern her. But it should; and if she thought more positively about herself it would.

When I was trying to get over Mr. Unavailable, friends and family provided an invaluable support system. My mother came to visit and cooked meals for me; a kind ex-boyfriend sent supplies of white chocolate. My nine-year-old nephew hid forty affectionate notes throughout my apartment: in my jacket pockets, beneath the chopping board, in the coffee grinder, among my cosmetics, in the linen closet, on the pot plants, in the breakfast cereal, underneath the flower vases, among the coasters . . . For weeks I would unexpectedly come across a colorful scrap of paper proclaiming, "Guess who loves you?"; "Adam loves you"; "Adam loves you—still!!!" (When I moved house a year later, there were five notes still undiscovered; I often wondered what the next tenants found . . . ) Girlfriends flew in for weekends; we pampered ourselves at spas, indulged ourselves in restaurants, treated ourselves in shops. We stayed in our pajamas all day and watched Jodie Foster movies. I played a lot of sports; I got eight hours' sleep; I redecorated my house. I started a weight-lifting program and viewed it as a metaphor: I was becoming *strong*.

Oh—and I read *All's Well That Ends Well*. I didn't want my story to end like Helen's.

~

*Two Noble Kinsmen* offers us a different conclusion to the problem of loving the man who doesn't love back. The jailer's daughter can't have, and doesn't get, Prince Arcite. Instead, she marries the local boy who has long loved her. We don't know if she is happy with this conclusion or just resigned to it. But there's a lot to be said in favor of accepting the good and gentle friend who loves you and is available, instead of obsessing with the prince who will never look in your direction.

But that is a different topic: acceptance, not obsession. Let's turn to that.

# Seven

# ACCEPTANCE

*I crave no other, nor no better man.*

—*Measure for Measure*

In real life, as in Shakespeare, outright villains are easy to avoid falling in love with. More difficult to resist are those men who are not villains but whose bad qualities outweigh their good. Shakespeare depicted three such bad boys, all of them in plays written in the middle of his career when the romance scenario was compromised by a heavy dose of "real life": *Troilus and Cressida*, *Measure for Measure*, and *All's Well That Ends Well*. The heroes in these plays are all flawed. Troilus is a narcissist; Angelo is a hypocrite; Bertram is immature. I've dated them all.

In fact I had one brief relationship where my partner was all three of the above. I don't know if this was an example of multitasking on my part (why have three bad relationships when you can have them all in one?). But so supreme a disaster area was this guy that my friends never used his name, referring to him solely, like a Spenserian allegory, as the Jerk.

How do you deal with the jerk? Mariana in *Measure for Measure* offers one approach.

Mariana has had a broken engagement to Angelo before the beginning of the play; Angelo dumped her when her family did not come up with the required dowry. In Shakespeare's day an engagement was a much stronger commitment than it is today, as binding as marriage; indeed, it was a form of marriage, lacking only consummation to make it permanent. Angelo's behavior is thus, by Elizabethan legal standards, appalling. Perhaps aware that you cannot easily break an engagement, Angelo compounds his crime with slander. His primary reason for reneging on his marital bond, he says, was not Mariana's financial insufficiency but "discoveries of dishonor" in her (3.1.227). Angelo's slander not only libels Mariana but effectively renders her unmarriageable: no Elizabethan male will court a woman whose honor has been compromised. Nor is this lie a desperate impromptu measure that he later repents: Angelo repeats it in public in act 5 ("her reputation was disvalued"; 5.1.221).

And why was Mariana dowerless? Because her brother was shipwrecked at sea "having in that perish'd vessel the dowry of his sister" (3.1.217). In one moment Mariana loses her brother, her dowry, and her betrothed husband. Angelo is impervious to her grief: he "left her in her tears, and dried not one of them with his comfort" (3.1.225–26). For five years Mariana has lived as a recluse. She has never recovered from Angelo's abandonment; she weeps daily. Pining for five years might come into the category of obsessive, addictive behavior. But as an abandoned betrothed woman Mariana has no future without Angelo.

Angelo's iniquitous behavior is just his *pre*-play activity. In the course of the play Angelo is shown to be a sexual harasser, a liar, a coward, and a hypocrite. As acting governor of Vienna during the duke's absence he operates a new-broom-sweeps-clean policy, insisting on capital punishment for premarital sex; yet he himself propositions and blackmails a novice nun, Isabella. As we saw in chapter 4, he promises to reprieve her condemned brother if she will have sex with him; if she won't agree, he will torture her brother and slander Isabella. (Calumny had worked with Mariana, so heck, why not try it again?) Isabella agrees to submit, but, unbeknown to Angelo, it is Mariana who appears in the bedroom. Despite Isabella's acquiescence, Angelo breaks his promise and condemns Claudio to death. (Breaking promises is something of a habit for Angelo.)

Accused in public in act 5, Angelo denies his deeds. Isabella lists his crimes: he is "forsworn," "a murderer," "an adulterous thief, / An hypocrite, a virgin-violator" (5.1.38–41). It's quite a CV. The old duke, newly returned, sentences Angelo to death. This is quid pro quo, or, in the play's New Testament parlance, "measure for measure." The man who condemned sexual transgressors is himself condemned.

Because she has slept with Angelo, Mariana is now fully Angelo's wife; his execution will make her a widow, and the duke wants her to be a *rich* widow. He confiscates Angelo's possessions, giving them to Mariana to "buy you a better husband" (5.1.425). Go for it, Mariana!

But Mariana refuses the duke's offer, arguing that "best men are moulded out of faults, / And for the most, become much more the better / For being a little bad; so may my husband" (5.1.439–41). I'm not happy about this reasoning: it anticipates a future reformed Angelo, one who can be changed ("moulded"), one who will change ("become . . . better"). You can't stake your happiness on the possibility of a partner changing his behavior. Nor am I sure that Angelo's peccadilloes fit the category of being "a little bad." In my book "a little bad" means forgetting to empty the dishwasher, staying out late in the pub, not putting your socks in the laundry basket; it doesn't include slander, broken promises, murder, hypocrisy.

But Mariana gives another reason for wanting to marry Angelo. When the duke offers her money and land to buy a better husband she refuses with the simple statement, "I crave no other, nor no better man" (5.1.426). Mariana here demonstrates, eloquently and movingly, an essential prerequisite for successful partnership: acceptance. You cannot hope to rescue your partner from his failings; you cannot hope to improve your partner's flaws. All you can do is accept them, and him. As Robin Norwood explains, "You must . . . let go of the idea that 'when he changes I'll be happy.' He may never change. You must stop trying to make him. *And you must learn to be happy anyway*" (my italics).

Mariana will never experience Helen's predicament in *All's Well*, loving an image, not a reality. Loving a jerk often overlaps with the problem of obsessive loving because one is in love with what the jerk might be (if he will allow himself to be saved by your love) or what you once thought he was before you found out he was a jerk. But Mariana has no illusions about Angelo. She does not see him as anything other than he is. Loving a flawed man is not a problem if you are happy to acknowledge that he is one. And maybe always will be.

This sounds simple but is far from it! It is easier to imagine that someone else will change, easier to wait for them to do so, than it is to accept them as they are. But no one will change just because you want them to; change can only come from within. A psychologist friend of mine makes this point in a joke. Q: "How many psychologists does it take to change a lightbulb?" A: "One. But the lightbulb must really, *really* want to change."

In my (rather old-fashioned) childhood it was a good-luck tradition for the bride to think of three church objects as she walked down the aisle on her wedding day. "Aisle—altar—hymn" were the items usually recommended by married female neighbors with a homonymic sense of humor. In the 1990s a hit comedy with the title *I Love You, You're Perfect, Now Change* ran on Broadway and in London's West End. Mariana's example is the opposite of these satiric sound bites. What she says is: "I love you, you're imperfect, that's OK." Such acceptance is an essential part of any viable long-term partnership.

I'm not suggesting that we accept abusers or murderers. But characters who are flawed, have limitations, who are a "little bad" (men or women): if we want to live with them, we must learn to love them as they are. In fact the ideal situation is one in which we love our partner *because* of his or her flaws not despite them.

The desire to change someone has a prior stage: judgment. You judge someone, you find them flawed, and so you want to change them. For whose benefit, I wonder? For theirs? Or for yours? In *Awareness* Tony de Mello reminds us that we cannot judge others, at least not in terms of what is good for them. How can we be the judge of that? (The only thing we can judge is whether they are good for us or not; but that is a completely different issue.)

Accepting someone is the opposite of judging them. It is a supremely spiritual concept. All religions advise their followers not to judge, and it is no accident that Mariana's acceptance brings to a close a play whose reprobate hero is a fallen angel (Angelo) and whose title comes from the sermon on the mount: "Judge not that you be not judged" (Matthew 7:1). A play about not judging is by definition a play about acceptance.

If we can't accept jerks, we must leave them. That is the course Cressida opts for in *Troilus and Cressida*. Tradition romanticizes Troilus as the betrayed lover, Cressida as the faithless woman. In fact, Troilus is a self-indulgent lover who thinks only of himself.

Troilus does not talk of love, although he talks much of passion and desire, nor does he talk of marriage to Cressida. He talks, as he thinks, of self and the senses. He wants to "wallow" in the lily beds of Cressida's environment (3.2.12). His "imaginary relish" is not of the spiritual but the sensual (3.2.18–29). Even as he and Cressida exchange confessions of love, he turns the conversation to himself. With six personal pronouns in thirteen lines (3.2.158–70), he extols his personal merits and belittles woman's constancy (and thus Cressida's)—a sobering start to any relationship. Not one of his romantic [sic] speeches can match the simple sincerity of Cressida's "I have lov'd you night and day / For many weary months" (3.2.114–15). And if we look ahead to act 4, we see how little substance there is behind his sentimental protestations.

In act 4 the Trojans announce that they will exchange Cressida (a Trojan whose father has defected to the Greeks) for a Trojan prisoner of war. Cressida is to be sent to the Greek camp immediately. Troilus makes no protestation, no denial (contrast Cressida's anguished and determined lines: "I will not go . . . I have forgot my father"; 4.2.94–96). His first thoughts are typically of himself: "how my achievements mock me!" (two personal pronouns in one line; 4.2.69). Is this all Cressida is to him—an "achievement"? His second thoughts are similarly unsentimental, a quick priming of the news bearer, Lord Aeneas, in protective mendacity: "and, my Lord Aeneas, / We met by chance, you did not find me here" (4.2.70–71). He exits; no thoughts of Cressida; no farewell; no comfort.

When Troilus returns two scenes later, it is as part of the official Trojan delegation to accompany Cressida to the Greek camp. The brief private good-bye with Cressida is embedded in an atmosphere of mistrust: five commands to "be true," which distress rather than reassure Cressida ("O heavens! 'be true' again?"), and prompt her most poignant cry, "O heavens, you love me not!" (4.4.82). Furthermore Troilus's language and attitude in leave-taking are as self-centered as they were in love-making. The separation is seen as affecting only him, as divine punishment for his love (4.4.24–27). His speech accepts an externally imposed conclusion to the relationship: "Chance . . . strangles our dear vows / Even in the birth of our own laboring breath" (4.4.33–38). Troilus clearly accepts that the relationship is over. Apparently one night's "sport" has satisfied his sense of "achievement."

As the scene continues we see the superficial nature of Troilus's understanding of love and of Cressida. He describes the Greeks' charms, charms that he fears will attract Cressida: singing, dancing, "sweet . . . talk," "subtile games." These are externals. Cressida's love looks not with the eyes but with the mind, as she revealed in act 1. Troilus now delivers a short sermon—six pious, pragmatic, and emotionally inappropriate lines on the subject of temptation (4.4.89–97)—before Cressida's faltering question, "My lord, will *you* be true?" (my emphasis; 4.4.101). So far, the conversation has comprised nothing but instructions for *Cressida*'s behavior. Troilus sidesteps a direct response to her question (a question that clearly asks for reassurance and love) with a return to arrogant self-advertisement: seven lines (4.4.102–8) talking about how he is constitutionally incapable of infidelity. He concludes, "Fear not my truth: the moral of my wit / Is 'plain and true'; there's all the reach of it" (4.4.107–8). This glibly dismissive rhyme is the last Troilus speaks to Cressida in the play.

I began to view Troilus critically the year I dated the modern Troilus, my very own Mr. Narcissist. He was an uncanny action replay of Shakespeare's jerk, so much so that spotting the parallels became a game for me (and a way of detaching from him). How long before he would turn a conversation to himself? How long before he would present himself, like Troilus, as a victim? How many times could I endure suspicious lectures on the men I would meet in his absence? When was he going to stop meeting me in secret? (And in case you're wondering: no, he wasn't married.) Troilus is fascinating to study in Shakespeare; he is really interesting to watch on stage; but I didn't want to live with his modern equivalent.

There is not a shred of evidence in the scenes between Troilus and Cressida that Troilus is truly in love with Cressida. She, I believe, goes off to the Greek camp with that heartbroken realization. "O heavens, you love me not!" is her last statement to Troilus, not an expression of fear but an interpretation of evidence.

The play ends with the two lovers parted forever. Cressida chooses against Troilus, albeit at considerable emotional cost. In the Greek camp she turns to her bodyguard Diomedes. He manipulates her by his anger and his threats to leave her. She submits to his advances, but changes her mind four times before finally, reluctantly, giving in. It's hard to give someone up just because you know they're no good. Cressida never falls out of love with Troilus; she just falls into reason. It is an act of courage, not of betrayal. Unique among Shakespearean heroines, she makes the decision to follow her head, not her heart. This does not guarantee her happiness, but it does guarantee emotional survival.

Shakespearean heroines don't always fall in love with heroes. Like us, Shakespeare's women can love seriously flawed men. What to do in this situation? You can love them or leave them. But you can't change them.

～

Troilus and Diomedes have something in common: both manipulate Cressida's behavior. Troilus does this through moral lecturing. Diomedes does it more insidiously: through anger (as we saw in chapter 5). Anger is a big problem in any relationship. Shakespeare offers advice about how to deal with this emotion, both when we encounter it in others and in ourselves. That is the subject of the next chapter.

# Eight

# ANGER

*Never anger / Made good guard for itself.*

—*Antony and Cleopatra*

I briefly dated a man who had a short fuse (let's call him Mr. Chide). He would raise his voice; he would storm out of the house. Doors were slammed; telephones were put down mid-conversation. His anger would be over in a short space of time—half an hour, an evening—replaced by romantic penitence (let's call him Mr. Jekyll-and-Chide). I, on the other hand, was shaken for days. Such sudden eruptions left me tense. Soon I found myself walking on eggshells wondering what inadvertent word or action (from me; from his family; from the world) would trigger the next outburst. Life became the emotional equivalent of passive smoking: for him, anger was cathartic; for me, it was toxic.

During this time I repeatedly thought of Desdemona. Here's why.

In act 4 of *Othello*, the eponymous hero berates his wife in public. Desdemona has been engaged in a conversation with Lodovico, a Venetian nobleman, about Othello's dismissal of his lieutenant Michael Cassio. The conversation aggravates Othello and he undermines Desdemona's innocent comments with sarcastic questions ("Are you sure of that?" "Indeed?") and frustrated exclamations ("Fire and brimstone"). This unexpected brusqueness perplexes Desdemona, who asks Lodovico, "is he angry?" (4.1.226; 238; 234; 235). Lodovico proffers a rational explanation for Othello's sudden anger: maybe the business letter that he has just received has upset him.

But both Lodovico and Desdemona are taken by surprise when Othello's anger escalates from words to action: he hits Desdemona. Lodovico is appalled: "this would not be believ'd in Venice / Though I should swear I saw't" (4.1.242–43). Desdemona is in tears and Lodovico asks Othello to comfort her: "make her amends; she weeps." Othello's response is further vituperation: he scorns Desdemona, accuses her, and manipulates her physically (the dialogue invites him to spin her round and round) before brusquely ordering her away: "hence, avaunt."

Othello's display of anger is so out of character that Lodovico asks in bewilderment "Is this the nature / Whom passion could not shake?" (4.1.265–66). Is this a new side of Othello, he wonders ("new-create"; 276), or has he always been this way ("is it his use?"; 274). The scene is as shocking for the theater audience as it is for the onstage audience, and modern productions usually place the interval here, allowing us twenty minutes to recover.

But Shakespeare hasn't finished with us yet. In the next scene Othello rages at Desdemona again; she registers dismay at the "fury in his words" (4.2.32). When he exits she confesses her inability to deal with anger:

Those that do teach young babes
Do it with gentle means and easy tasks.
He might have chid me so; for in good faith
I am a child to chiding. (4.2.111–14)

It is a supremely reasonable statement: if she has done something to upset Othello, and if he wishes to point this out to her, he could do it gently. He does not need to get angry; she is inexperienced ("a child") in handling anger ("chiding"). *Chiding* was a very strong word in Shakespeare's day, meaning a loud and angry altercation.

Throughout my relationship with Mr. Chide I thought of Desdemona's words. Why doesn't Mr. Chide rebuke with "gentle means and easy tasks," I wondered. I didn't know how to deal with anger. Like Desdemona I was a stranger to anger, "a child to chiding."

In fact, I have never been comfortable with anger. I know someone who expresses her anger with a series of sniffs and sotto voce comments (Ms. Running Aside). Another acquaintance conveys her anger with sneering sarcasm (Ms. Snide). I find this as hard to handle as the outbursts of Mr. Chide. Part of the difficulty is that my reactions are somatic (I feel with my stomach), but part of it is that I feel demeaned as a rational human being: if there's a problem, why can't he or she state it and we can try to resolve it?

When I met my husband I had just turned forty. One of the things that happens when you fall in love as a mature adult is that you are far less likely to allow passion to overcome reason. You know what you can and cannot respect in a partner, almost to the point of having a checklist: is he a Freemason? Is he politically Conservative? Does he have kids? (In case you're wondering, these were all questions to which I wanted a *negative* answer.) At the time we met, there was one question that mattered to me above all others: "What makes you angry?" He hesitated for ages before saying, almost apologetically, as if it were a deficiency, "I can't really think of anything." Right answer! More-than-right answer! In fact: Mr. Right!

I know that anger can be an attractive quality to some. It expresses passion and creates excitement and drama; consequently, fiery temperaments can be magnetic. In *Twelfth Night* Olivia sighs, "O what a deal of scorn looks beautiful / In the contempt and anger of his lip" (3.1.145–46); just two lines later she declares her love for this angry youth, Cesario. In *As You Like It* Rosalind (in disguise as a boy) realizes that Phoebe has fallen in love with "my anger" (3.5.67). I know that anger is human. Timon of Athens acknowledges that "to be in anger is impiety; / But who is man that is not angry?" (3.5.56–57). I know that anger can be healthy. People who repress anger often fall in love with those who flare up easily; they thus manage to experience vicariously this normal emotion. I know that sex after an argument is supposed to be great—although personally I can think of better forms of foreplay. My issue is not with the emotion itself but with the outlets for that emotion; not with anger but with ways of expressing anger.

Certainly, anger needs to be expressed. If you deny it an outlet, the body will seek another way to express it: physical illness, depression, pathologically passive-aggressive behavior (which is simply an accumulation of anger expressed at a later stage for no immediate reason). In *The Taming of the Shrew*, Katherine, the vocal woman whom society wishes to silence, utters a heartfelt defense of her need to express her anger:

> My tongue will tell the anger of my heart,
> Or else my heart concealing it will break. (4.3.77–78)

Speech is essential for her emotional survival, she says. This is, I think, one of the most wrenching statements in Shakespeare. Katherine does not want to act angrily, to kick and spit (as stage productions often make her do); she is simply asking to be heard, to *tell* her anger, to protest against the status quo. This is assertion, not aggression. And assertion is one of the healthiest expressions of anger. (A lot of self-help literature is aimed at helping meek people to become more assertive. But angry people need to acquire this skill too, to learn how to convert aggression into assertion.)

Anger is good when, like Katherine's, it challenges injustice. Such anger can be expressed creatively through petitions, letters of protest, phone calls to government officials, running for public office, founding support groups, or doing volunteer work. In *1 Henry VI* Shakespeare uses a digestive metaphor in an unusual transitive sense (with an object) to show the benefit of converting anger to outward action. The king instructs his factious nobles: "digest / Your angry choler on your enemies" (4.1.167–68). (Technically this is not *ex*pression of anger but *sup*pression followed by redirection, a two-part stage known to psychologists as "conversion.") By redirecting their anger the nobles will not consume ("digest") themselves; conversion prevents anger from turning inward and becoming self-destructive.

If anger turned inward is damaging, so is anger that is nurtured and turns to hate or revenge. In a prayer to the heavens in *King Lear* Lear asks first for patience and then for "noble anger" (2.4.276). What is noble anger? Lear seems to think of it as manly action, the opposite of useless tears (which he calls "women's weapons, water-drops"; 2.4.277). But in the next sentence he makes clear that the noble anger he anticipates is revenge: "I will have such revenges on you both . . ." (2.4.279). At this point, my heart sinks.

Revenge is something we associate with bygone ages. With the ethical codes of earlier societies, which saw human life as cheap and expendable. With the retaliations of Greek or Roman or Renaissance tragedy. With the atrocities of Seneca's Thyestes and Shakespeare's Titus Andronicus, both of whom kill their enemy's sons, bake them in a pie, and serve them at a banquet to their unsuspecting parents. (Today's special? *Fils en croute.*)

But revenge is all too prevalent today. We see it every time a newspaper bays for the blood of a convicted criminal or publishes "name and shame" lists of offenders. We see it when people protest against the release of convicted criminals and express outrage at the lenience of prison sentences or the cost of rehabilitation. We see it when campaigners argue for the restoration of the death penalty on the grounds of an eye-for-an-eye ethic.

"Nothing can bring back my son/daughter/husband/wife" we hear. True. But how does revenge help? As Martin Luther King Jr. famously said, an eye-for-an-eye philosophy leaves everyone blind.

Revenge is an expression of anger, of pain, of injustice. And while some expressions of anger can be positive and constructive, revenge is not one of them.

～

Because of the surge of adrenaline that facilitates all animals' "fight or flight" reactions, human beings become physically stronger when they are angry. In *2 Henry VI* the duke of York fulminates, "O, I could hew up rocks and fight with flint, / I am so angry" (5.1.24–25). It is this extra physical strength that makes loss of control when you are angry so dangerous: it may lead to impulsive physical assault. *Cymbeline* describes the opposite effect.

When a fight is reported between two characters, the queen asks in alarm if any harm was done. A servant replies:

> There might have been,
> But that my master rather play'd than fought
> And had no help of anger. (1.1.161–63)

Without the energy surge that comes from anger, a fight is not dangerous, mere play.

If one adds alcohol to anger, one has a dangerous combination. In *Henry V* we are told that Alexander the Great killed his best friend "in his rages, and his furies, and his wraths, and his cholers, and his moods, and his displeasures, and his indignations, and also being a little intoxicates in his prains [brains], . . . in his ales and his angers" (4.7.34–38). The sentence is composed entirely of synonyms: the main ingredient is anger with the later tragic addition of alcohol to the adrenaline. Since alcohol leads to lack of control, and anger is itself a lack of control, together they deliver a double whammy. No wonder that metaphor often conflates the two, as in *1 Henry IV* where the angry Hotspur is "drunk with choler" (1.3.129).

Harry Hotspur is more often hotheaded (as his name indicates) than outright angry but we can learn a lot about anger by watching Hotspur's behavior in his first appearance in *1 Henry IV* where his anger gets in the way of effective communication. The king forbids Hotspur ever to mention the name of Mortimer (Hotspur's brother-in-law), whom the king accuses of being a traitor: "revolted Mortimer" (1.3.92).

He exits and Hotspur lets rip. His speeches have an escalating fury, repeating points with increasingly hyperbolic fantasies of petty revenge. Speak of Mortimer? He *will* speak of him. In fact he might well join him; he will even shed all his blood on behalf of Mortimer; he will raise Mortimer as high as the king (1.3.130–37). The king doesn't want to hear Mortimer's name? Well then, Hotspur will "find him when he lies asleep, / And in his ear [he'll] hollow [make a halloo sound] 'Mortimer!'" Furthermore, "I'll have a starling shall be taught to speak / Nothing but 'Mortimer,' and give it him" (1.3.221–25). It takes 100 lines of dialogue for Hotspur to say this (1.3.130–230): with tunnel vision he repeats the point furiously.

His uncle, the earl of Worcester, realizes that Hotspur is carried away by rage and rebukes him. Worcester now turns to political business. "Those same noble Scots / That are your prisoners—" he begins, but Hotspur interrupts him: "I'll keep them all!" Hotspur then repeats this point with a rising tone: "By God, he [the king] shall not have a Scot of them." Then adamantly: "No, if a Scot would save his soul, he shall not!" And again: "I'll keep them, by this hand!" (1.3.213–16). It has taken Hotspur four lines to say (and repeat) one point, a point that Worcester does not wish to contest: "Those prisoners you shall keep" (217). But in his anger Hotspur is not paying attention: "Nay, I will," he insists, "that's flat" (218). What does "nay" mean here? There is nothing to contradict.

Hotspur's anger prevents communication. As he becomes more and more heated, his speech becomes more and more extravagant, and the conversation goes nowhere. His rhetorical wheels are spinning.

This display of anger is exasperating (and time wasting) but is probably not harmful. Nonetheless, the failure in communication and the belligerent repetition, characteristic of angry personalities, epitomize Hotspur throughout. He lacks self-control.

Loss of self-control, either verbal (saying things you regret) or physical (violence) is harmful in anger because it damages relationships. Things said cannot be unsaid; violence prevents future trust. Seneca, the Stoic philosopher, described anger as a form of temporary madness because the angry person is out of control. But losing control has another consequence: it makes you look silly. (This is why the scenes in which Hotspur appears are comic.) In life displays of anger are meant to demonstrate the angry person's moral superiority. In fact, losing your temper just makes you look foolish. Getting heated isn't cool.

Once others realize that the angry person lacks self-control, they have an advantage. In *Antony and Cleopatra* Augustus Caesar is rattled by Antony's displays of anger. Antony is verbally abusive to Caesar ("He calls me boy, and chides as he had power / To beat me out of Egypt" complains Caesar; 4.1.1–2). He is physically abusive to Caesar's messenger ("My messenger / He hath whipt with rods"; 4.1.2–3). He challenges Caesar ("dares me to personal combat"; 4.1.3). However, Caesar's wise counselor Maecenas pacifies Caesar by telling him how to interpret this kind of behavior: "When one so great begins to rage, he's hunted / Even to falling [that is, his anger shows that he's desperate]" (4.1.7–8).

In *Henry VIII* Shakespeare uses an equestrian image to show how anger gets you nowhere. Norfolk advises his friend, Buckingham, to analyze what he is trying to achieve with anger:

> Stay, my lord,
> And let your reason with your choler question
> What 'tis you go about: to climb steep hills
> Requires slow pace at first. Anger is like
> A full hot [very high-spirited] horse, who, being allow'd his way,
> Self-mettle [his own energy] tires him. (1.1.129–34)

In other words: take it calmly if you want to get anywhere. (Or, in the immortal words of Bart Simpson: "Don't have a cow, man!")

Buckingham is not persuaded, however. He says that he is going to make a fuss, and a public fuss at that, about what is bothering him. Norfolk's response reveals him to be not merely a pacifist but a strategist: "Be advis'd; / Heat not a furnace for your foe so hot / That it do singe yourself." He continues this advice in an elegant variant of the standard hare-versus-tortoise argument: "We may outrun / By violent swiftness that which we run at, / And lose by overrunning." Then he offers an aphoristic variant: "The fire that mounts the liquor till't run o'er / In seeming to augment it wastes it [that is, heat makes things rise but it also boils them over; then what have you gained?]." He compliments Buckingham, saying that Buckingham is actually the best person to achieve what he wants "if with the sap of reason [he] would quench, / Or but allay, the fire of passion" (1.1.139–49). Anger is consistently opposed to reason; one response is intemperate, the other is not.

For Buckingham anger is a "disease" (1.1.125). And the remedy he offers for being chafed, choleric, passionate—all Elizabethan synonyms for angry—is "temp'rance [patience]" (1.1.124). Iago says the same thing when he describes a woman who "being ang'red" and "her revenge being nigh" (note the invidious sequence—anger leads to revenge) "bade her wrong stay, and her displeasure fly" (2.1.152–53). That is, she resolved to put up with her wrong patiently. Easier said than done, of course. (To see how to achieve this you'll need to turn to chapter 11, on forgiveness.) But the point here is that whereas angry people often think their behavior impressive and effective, the world knows otherwise. The sensible Maecenases and Buckinghams of the world view the angry person as *less* impressive and effective for his anger. In fact, Maecenas makes a practical observation that ought to become a proverb: "Never anger / Made good guard for itself" (*Antony and Cleopatra* 4.1.9–10). In other words, anger is not a good protection or bodyguard.

～ᗡ

And what about women who are angry? I have been talking so far as if anger is a unisex phenomenon both in vocal expression and in society's sanctioned outlets. This is not the case. Women express anger differently from men. When I'm irritated with my husband for some minor misdemeanor that I view as a heinous crime (being late, for instance), I express it with silence (Ms. Access Denied). But men *love* silence! (For an eloquent exploration of male/female anger, and how to communicate, see John Gray's *Men Are from Mars, Women Are from Venus*.)

I recently overheard a woman berate a car-rental official at Dulles International Airport for failing to provide the child car seat that she had ordered. She was visibly, audibly, dramatically angry, and the elderly couple behind me in the queue expressed disquiet at such "unfeminine" behavior. But concepts of feminine and masculine are partly related to social conditioning. Car-Seat Lady was simply expressing her anger in ways that men have long allowed themselves to do.

Historically men's outlets for anger have been physical: they can do athletic sports, join the army, shoot people. (As the popular saying has it: "When women get angry they go shopping; men invade a foreign country.") The discrepancy between what society allows men and women in the way of outlets for anger is one of the themes of *The Taming of the Shrew*. Katherine, the shrew of the title, is an angry woman who protests vocally. She protests, as far as I can make out, about her society's gender stereotyping: her sister's "silence flouts me, / And I'll be reveng'd" (2.1.29). In other words, she dislikes the thoughtless binary that stereotypes women as either mild, silent, and therefore marriageable (like her sister) or talkative, shrewish, and therefore unmarriageable (like herself).

Her rough suitor, Petruchio, is a physically and verbally violent man: he strikes his servants, swears in church, and carouses with the communion wine. What would we call him if he were a woman? After hearing of Petruchio's violent ill temper in act 4, a servant concludes "By this reck'ning he is more shrew than she" (4.1.85).

At the start of the play, Petruchio alludes to an earlier career as a soldier. He offers credentials from his military curriculum vitae as evidence that he will be able to endure a "woman's tongue" (line 207). But his references remind us that society provides organized outlets for male aggression; society has ways of legitimizing male anger. In Shakespeare's time there were no outlets for female anger, physical or verbal, as Katherine unhappily realizes.

Women now have verbal and physical outlets for anger. I recently saw a TV program about road rage in which the psychologist-presenter prescribed preventive measures for irascible drivers. A young woman was sent to boxing lessons so that she could get rid of her aggression before getting behind the wheel. (And where was I when I was watching this program? On the Concept 2 rower in the gym after a particularly irritating committee meeting.)

During our brief relationship, Mr. Chide explained to me that his storming out of the house and slamming down the telephone were tactics that enabled him to handle his rage: they distanced him from the situation and prevented his anger from escalating. I am glad that these tactics worked for him; they never worked for me, and never will. The reason they don't is because they are used manipulatively. They create a one-way relationship in which the fiery person will be dominant because the pacifist partner will try to appease. Everyone wants things to go their way but angry people become angry when their demands are not met. (It is a myth that it is good to let rip. That is simply a euphemism for getting in touch with your inner two-year-old.)

My way of handling Mr. Chide's anger was to write about it academically. I wrote a reproachful article about angry male characters in *Troilus and Cressida*; a Shakespeare journal rejected it on the grounds that it was "strangely accusatory." Indeed it was; it was do-it-yourself therapy, not academic criticism. A few years later I revised it and it was published in a Renaissance journal devoted to "Performing Anger." "Perform" comes from the Latin *perfurnire* and means to carry through to an end, to complete, to conclude. The article brought closure to my relationship with Mr. Chide.

Some are born angry (those who constitutionally have a low tolerance for frustration). Some develop anger (traumatic memories can cause delayed expressions of anger). Some have anger thrust upon them (those who live with aggressive people). Shakespeare has advice for all three parties.

1. Prevent anger with good communication. Learn from Hotspur. In *1 Henry IV* this angry character doesn't listen (like Falstaff in the sequel, *2 Henry IV*, he has the "malady of not marking"; 1.2.122). Hotspur's behavior in the political scenes is paralleled in the personal scenes with his wife where he deliberately and impetuously misunderstands and misinterprets her. I wouldn't want to have a conversation with this man. I wouldn't want to date him either.

2. Defuse anger with humor. This works for both the angry party—who can learn to laugh at him/herself—and for the partner, who can prevent situations from escalating with a loving tease. The sources of anger, when scrutinized, are often sources of humor. But beware the angry humor that has developed into cynicism. I wouldn't want to date the cynical, witty Jacques in *As You Like It*. (However, he wouldn't want to date me either—he abhors the coupling at the play's end.)

3. Defeat anger with logic. Logic is rational; anger is not. (See Norfolk's conversation with Buckingham, above.)

4. Use your imagination. This is Shakespeare's advice in all situations (psychologists would call it cognitive restructuring). Changing the way you think changes how you act (and react). This applies to both the angry partner and the one on the receiving end. Mr. Chide's anger was his emotional reaction to external events. My reaction to his anger was fear. (Others might react with retaliation, hostility, defensive argument.) Instead of crumbling, I trained myself to imagine what underlay his anger: frustration, neglect, vulnerability, pain, uncertainty, jealousy. Failing to read between the lines is a common Shakespearean problem. (We saw it spectacularly, tragically illustrated by King Lear, for example, in chapter 2, "Family.") Imagining events from the other's point of view can offer prevention or solution. In other words: "See better."

Using my imagination to see things from Mr. Chide's point of view helped me a lot. But by then I had discovered something else: my own needs and limitations. Unwilling to contemplate a life of vicarious anger, of sympathetic projection, I opted out.

I learned how to handle Mr. Chide's anger only to realize I didn't want to. Some skills are best kept for emergencies.

Othello's anger, with which we began this chapter, was linked to jealousy. Like Mr. Chide's it was an expression of vulnerability and insecurity. Jealousy is a big topic—let's give it a chapter to itself.

# Nine

# JEALOUSY

*O, beware, my lord, of jealousy! /*
*It is the green-ey'd monster.*

—*Othello*

All relationships entail the prospect of loss. Jealousy is simply the constant anticipation of loss. What a simple explanation—a one-sentence definition! But in practice jealousy and its effects are far from straightforward. For one thing, jealousy often leads to physical and emotional abuse. For another, it is difficult to cure without professional help. But understanding the causes of jealousy can prevent things getting to the stage where jealousy ruins the relationship.

I once had a colleague whose long-distance boyfriend suffered from jealousy. This meant my colleague suffered too. She couldn't have a drink with male colleagues without arousing her boyfriend's suspicion. At conferences she couldn't speak to old friends without being watched. She was cross-examined after social gatherings. When they were together at parties her conversation with other men was actually *timed*. Determined to maintain a normal life she continued to jog or see films with male friends and colleagues but concealed these innocuous events. Inevitably they were discovered and all hell broke loose. It was a vicious spiral: his jealousy provoked her furtive behavior, which he then treated as evidence of the one thing it wasn't—guilt.

The jealous partner will always find the evidence he or she needs to support his or her suspicions. Having one's worst fears confirmed is less painful than living in suspicion. Certainty is more bearable than uncertainty. And if the facts do not support certainty, the jealous partner will manufacture it. Watching his wife lean conversationally toward Polixenes in *The Winter's Tale*, Leontes asks, "Is whispering nothing? / Is leaning cheek to cheek?" (1.2.284–85), to which the rational answer is: maybe, maybe not; who knows? But he concludes, "Why then the world and all that's in't is nothing." For him, there is no halfway house: either there is evidence of Hermione's guilt, or there is nothing. By act 3, as critic Sam Thompson points out, Leontes "has abandoned any attempt to defeat uncertainty by discovering the objective facts of his situation" and declares fact to be "merely what he says it is."

Love, as Shakespeare says in *A Midsummer Night's Dream*, is a transforming emotion: "Things base and vile, holding no quantity / Love can transform to form and dignity" (1.1.232–33). Jealousy is also a transforming emotion but in the other direction. It reverses the quotation: it turns "dignity" into "things base and vile." Both love and jealousy "look not with the eyes but with the mind" (*A Midsummer Night's Dream* 1.1.234), but love does so positively, jealousy perversely.

Sexual jealousy is, then, like most problems in Shakespeare, a failure to see things correctly. In *A Midsummer Night's Dream*, when Oberon accuses his wife, Titania, of loving Theseus, he cites as evidence her interference in Theseus's love affairs. Titania rejects the accusation: "These are the forgeries of jealousy" (*A*

*Midsummer Night's Dream* 2.1.81). *Forgeries*: fabrications, fictions, inventions; imagination gone wrong. Jealousy is indeed a forgery of imagination. It is a perversion of facts, a manipulation of reality. *A Midsummer Night's Dream* shows the power of imagination to create a new reality, to grow to "something of great constancy" (5.1.26), whether in the mechanicals' world of drama or in the lovers' hearts; but Titania's statement here reminds us of the negative potential of imagination. As Theseus explains a few lines earlier: "In the night, imagining some fear, / How easy is a bush suppos'd a bear" (5.1.21–22). The jealous lover inhabits an emotional "night": in imagining his worst fear he constantly mistakes bushes for bears.

~

The Shakespeare canon offers three striking examples of sexual jealousy: *The Merry Wives of Windsor*, *Othello*, and *The Winter's Tale*. *The Merry Wives* is one of Shakespeare's greatest comedies, a farce about domestic life. The plot revolves round the increasingly extreme attempts of the jealous Mr. Ford to catch his faithful wife in flagrante delicto with Falstaff.

Mistress Ford does indeed encourage Falstaff's advances but only so that she may teach him a lesson. One such lesson involves hiding Falstaff in the laundry basket ("buck-basket"); Mistress Ford instructs her servants to carry the basket to the Thames and dump its contents in the river. Ford takes this concealment of Falstaff as proof of his wife's infidelity and becomes comically apoplectic. He fulminates to himself: "There's a hole made in your best coat, Master Ford. This 'tis to be married! This 'tis to have linen and buck-baskets!" (3.5.141–43).

Ford's images here are of ownership gone wrong. Someone has damaged his best coat; for him marriage is equated with material possessions, with "linen and buck-baskets," like some metaphoric version of IKEA. But if you think of marriage as ownership and of your wife as property, you will live with the fear of *lost* property.

In Elizabethan times wives were legally the husband's property. As Petruchio says of his wife Katherine in *The Taming of the Shrew:*

> She is my goods, my chattels, she is my house,
> My household stuff, my field, my barn,
> My horse, my ox, my ass, my any thing. (3.2.230–32)

The sheer length of the list, with its ten items and exaggerated details, punctures its claim to seriousness and shows Shakespeare's skepticism about marriage as ownership. (See chapter 12 for the way in which Shakespeare recasts vocabulary of ownership to present a positive view of marriage as joint investment in *The Merchant of Venice*.) Today we no longer have the concept of marriage as legal ownership; but some people still have a concept of *emotional* ownership. And where there is ownership, there can be loss.

*The Merry Wives* ends, as comedy should, with characters reformed. Mr. Ford has the "figures" (figments of his imagination) "scrape[d]" out of his "brains" (4.2.216). Things do not end so happily in other genres: in the tragicomic world of *The Winter's Tale* or in the tragic world of *Othello*. In both these plays jealousy is made more complex by being situation specific: it is placed within pregnancy in *The Winter's Tale* and within a mixed marriage in *Othello*.

In *The Winter's Tale* Leontes observes his wife Hermione behaving hospitably to a houseguest, Polixenes, and immediately suspects her of having an affair. Never mind that Polixenes is Leontes' oldest friend. Never mind that Leontes himself invited

Polixenes to visit. Never mind that Leontes specifically asked Hermione to spend time with Polixenes to persuade Polixenes to extend his visit. All that matters is the situation: Hermione is pregnant.

Pregnant women, then and now, may experience many difficulties but they have one advantage over men: they always know who is the mother of their child! Men do not enjoy the same certainty in paternity. Consequently, men who are otherwise free from sexual suspicion can display signs of jealousy when their partners become pregnant. So prevalent is the phenomenon that psychologists sometimes call it the "Leontes syndrome." Like jealousy in general, this jealousy is an expression of vulnerability and insecurity.

Polixenes has been on vacation at Leontes' court for nine months—a length of time that now seems to Leontes suspiciously significant. Leontes is not just a Jacobean patriarch (in whose culture legitimacy was crucial) but a king, so legitimacy is doubly important to him. As his jealousy takes hold, it comes to apply not just to his unborn child but retrospectively to his young son, Mamillius. Leontes anxiously asks if his son looks like him, seeking reassurance of the boy's legitimacy. (It is perhaps no coincidence that this play uses so many metaphors taken from printing. Is the new technology of printing the only form of reproduction in which Jacobean males can have confidence?)

In *The Winter's Tale* Leontes puts his wife on trial, sentences her to death, and abandons the baby girl to whom she gives birth. Because the play is technically a comedy (or at least an averted tragedy—a tragicomedy) the baby girl survives and is brought up by shepherds. Hermione is not killed but, unbeknown to Leontes, lives in hiding for sixteen years. The family is eventually reunited. However, damage has been done: sixteen years of lost family life cannot be reinstated. (In a recent production, Hermione was portrayed as overjoyed to be reunited with her daughter yet she shunned her husband. Shakespeare's dialogue does not provide any lines for her to address to Leontes.)

Like Leontes, Othello's situation makes him particularly vulnerable to the "green-eyed monster." Othello is much older than his bride. The marriage is interracial (Othello is black, his wife, Desdemona, is white). Other factors make the situation more precarious and volatile: Desdemona is Venetian (Venetian women were famous for their promiscuity in the Elizabethan era. Iago's explanation that "in Venice they do let God see the pranks / They dare not show their husbands" was a stereotype that held much credit; 3.3.202–3). Iago, Othello's ensign (standard-bearer in his regiment), exploits these facts. He plays on all of Othello's vulnerabilities: his inexperience in the ways of Venice, his love for Desdemona, and his fear of losing her (to a white man, to a younger man).

Othello does in the end lose Desdemona, but it is because he kills her, not because she is unfaithful (which she is not). Othello then commits suicide, and his dying words provide not only his own obituary but a character description of every jealous lover: "one that lov'd not wisely but too well" (5.2.344).

Before we reach this tragic conclusion, Desdemona, baffled at Othello's anger toward her, has a conversation with her waiting woman, Emilia. Emilia realizes that Othello's behavior is that of a jealous man and says as much. Desdemona is astonished—"Alas the day, I never gave him cause." Emilia's answer is psychologically astute:

> But jealous souls will not be answer'd so.
> They are not ever jealous for the cause,

> But jealous for they're jealous. It is a monster
> Begot upon itself, born on itself. (3.4.159–62)

Don't waste your time looking for a rational explanation. Jealousy has no source; it is its own source.

This is true of another affliction—racism. It seems to me no accident that Shakespeare has coupled a story of jealousy with a story of racism. They are parallel conditions.

Samuel Taylor Coleridge would disagree, of course. In the nineteenth century he inaugurated a view, still influential today, that Iago, Othello's ensign, suffers from "motiveless malignancy." It is true that Iago plots against Othello for no discernible reason (although he offers us several in soliloquy, all different and unconvincing). But the point is surely that racism does not have a reason or an origin. It does not require a source; it is its own origin. Like jealousy, it is "a monster begot upon itself, born on itself." As the English essayist Sydney Smith said, "Never try to reason the prejudice out of a man. It was not reasoned into him."

At the beginning of the play, Othello is called to the senate in the middle of the night. Othello is a respected military leader in Venice and the duke now needs his help in thwarting an unexpected Turkish invasion. As it happens, this is Othello's wedding night: he has just married Desdemona without the knowledge of Desdemona's father, Brabantio. When the wedding is revealed to the assembled council, Brabantio objects vociferously and disowns his daughter. We see here a particularly pernicious kind of racism: you can serve our city but you can't marry our daughters. Although Brabantio has regularly invited Othello to his home and accepted him as a prominent and admired military leader, he cannot accept him as a son-in-law.

The Elizabethans equated black skin color with the devil, and hence with moral blackness. In medieval plays the devil was portrayed as black. In the Elizabethan printing house the printer's assistant, covered in ink dust, was known familiarly as the "printer's devil." The duke fortunately sees beyond skin color, pointing out to Brabantio that Othello's "virtue" makes him "far more fair than black" (1.3.289–90), and Desdemona reveals that she saw Othello's "visage in his mind" (1.3.252). Brabantio nonetheless remains unreconciled to his daughter's choice of husband.

However, Othello's position is even more complicated than variant skin color, as the play's subtitle, *The Moor of Venice*, reveals. Moors do not come from Italy; they come from North Africa. "The Moor of Venice" is an oxymoron. Othello is doubly an outsider in the play because of color and nationality. It is this that makes him so vulnerable to Iago's manipulations. When Iago tells Othello that he is ignorant of Venetian customs and of the promiscuity of Venetian women, Othello believes him.

If we are in any doubt that *Othello* is a play about racism we need look no further than Iago's name. Iago is the name of the patron saint of Spain, famous for overthrowing the Moors in 939 B.C.E., and well known to the Elizabethans. In Shakespeare's source, an Italian novella by Giraldo Cinthio called *Hecatommithi* (1565), Othello's ensign is nameless. Shakespeare could not have chosen a name so loaded with cultural baggage by accident. Iago hates Moors; that is what the name Iago means.

Iago is also a jealous husband. Emilia tells him that his intelligence has been turned "the seamy side without" (4.2.146) because he has suspected her sexually with Othello. His two paranoid suspicions come together here: he fears losing his wife to another; and he fears the foreign in the form of a visibly different human.

*Othello* ends in tragedy for many reasons—sexual jealousy, insecurity, miscommunication, racism. Iago exploits racial difference for his own ends. In this play, as in life, the human mind is the problem, not skin color. But it is the human mind that makes skin color a problem. (Racism, as someone once said, is a pigment of the imagination.) Like jealousy it is self-generated, it is a "forgery" of the imagination. "See better."

Valentine explains in *The Two Gentlemen of Verona* that "love, thou know'st, is full of jealousy" (2.4.177). He's wrong. It is attachment that is full of jealousy. Insecurity is full of jealousy. Jealous people may love their partner but their feelings of insecurity compromise and override love, reality, and evidence. It is an impossible situation. Understanding the partner's vulnerability may help us deal with the jealousy and thus enable both the suspected partner and the relationship to survive. Psychologists tell us that although the jealous partner cannot be cured, the *couple* can be helped. In counseling, my colleague learned that her long-distance boyfriend's shock when his first wife left him for another man had made him suspicious of everyone. He needed constant reassurance. He felt vulnerable when she was with male colleagues or friends. Like Hamlet, or Posthumus in *Cymbeline*, his disgust with one woman had become a general suspicion of womankind. (Hamlet equates all women with infidelity: "Frailty, thy name is woman!" (1.2.146); Posthumus rants that all men must be bastards if they are born to women.) The jealous partner must learn to trust (or in the case of Posthumus and of my colleague's boyfriend, trust again).

Trust does not provide a guarantee of anything—as we will

see in chapter 12, all relationships involve risk. But no one can live in constant anticipation of loss.

Many of the problems we have been examining in this book are problems of excess. Loving too much, like Helen or Othello ("one that loved not wisely but too well"); having too much anger (like Hotspur or Iago); speaking too much (like Katherine) or not enough (like Cordelia). Excess is always a problem in Shakespeare. It is the root of Shakespearean comedy and tragedy alike. As critics point out, in tragedy excess leads to disaster; in comedy it has to be put right.

Shakespeare often thinks of emotional excess in dietary terms. Overburdened by bad news in *The Two Gentlemen of Verona*, Valentine exclaims "I have *fed* upon this woe already, / And now *excess* of it will make me *surfeit*" (3.1.221–22; my emphasis). This is the same vocabulary as that of Orsino in *Twelfth Night*, who has a bulimic attitude to love:

> If music be the food of love, play on,
> Give me excess of it, that surfeiting [that is, overeating to the
>     point of being nauseated]
> The appetite may sicken [that is, vomit], and so die. (1.1.1–3)

His emetic philosophy might seem a bit over the top but that sets the appropriate tone for a play that is concerned with excess.

All the characters in *Twelfth Night* suffer from excess of some kind. Orsino is excessively in love (and he loves someone who doesn't love back—see chapter 6). The object of his devotion, the countess Olivia, is excessively in mourning: she has vowed to perform thrice-daily rituals of weeping as a tribute to her dead brother and to commemorate him by mourning for seven years. (In Shakespeare's time there was no "set" period of mourning; three days to a week was considered adequate and up to a year was considered possible, although this period was rarely achieved.) There is as much narcissistic self-indulgence in this behavior as there is in Orsino's persistent unrequited love.

Mourning is not the only example of excessive behavior in Olivia's household. The steward, Malvolio, is excessively egotistical: Olivia tells him, in a dietary metaphor that is now familiar to us in the play, "You are *sick* of self-love, Malvolio, and *taste* with a distemp'red *appetite*" (1.5.90–91; my emphasis). Olivia's uncle, the reprobate Sir Tony, refuses to "confine [him]self within the modest limits of order" (1.3.8–9); his eating, drinking, and reveling are over the top. With Olivia's observation that "he's in the third degree of drink, he's drown'd" (1.5.135–36), the literal shipwreck that began the play recurs metaphorically: Toby drowns in excess. Metaphors of food and drink, of overeating and overdrinking, of floating and drowning, merge as the characters shun moderation in diet, in love, and in life. Oscar Wilde's later rejection of moderation, with its imagery of excess and eating, could have been meant as a summary of *Twelfth Night*: "Enough is as bad as a meal. More than enough is as good as a feast."

Shakespeare is the champion of moderation. His recurrent metaphors for balanced emotions and a balanced life come from food.

I am not a creature of moderation. I love to eat. I am permanently hungry. As I eat one meal I am already planning what the next will be. I travel with emergency supplies in my handbag. By "supplies" I don't mean bars of chocolate; I mean hard-boiled eggs, yogurt, bananas, miniature meals (for two). I try not to be embarrassed when I go through airport security.

Once, when we had just moved house, I was more than usually hungry after a day of physical labor. Waiting for my husband at the local Indian restaurant, I ordered for two but, as 9:30 p.m. became 10 p.m., hunger overtook restraint; I ate my meal, then started on Peter's. By the time he arrived I had finished both. The waiter passed my table and said, slowly, "That's an awful lot of food for one person." I like to think he said this in awe, amazed at the sheer Falstaffian life force that had dispatched two meals with such relish.

But on second thought I don't think I'll take Falstaff as a role model. In the *Henry IV* plays this famous glutton is contrasted with the royals, Henry IV and Prince Hal, who know how to control their appetites. Henry IV appears to his subjects in carefully rationed portions, he says, and thus whets his subjects' appetite for more of him because he seems "like a feast" (*1 Henry IV* 3.2.59). This restraint is in deliberate contrast to the excesses of his predecessor, King Richard II, who was "daily swallowed by men's eyes," and so caused his subjects to overdose on him ("they surfeited with honey"). Hence, they grew to "loathe the taste of sweetness" (3.2.70, 73).

Like Richard, the rebel Hotspur and the anarchic Falstaff overindulge: Hotspur is drunk with anger and hungry for honor, and Falstaff indulges his appetite for food and drink in both tavern and battlefield. In the *Henry IV* plays dietary excess reflects a self-indulgence that does not foresee political consequences. In contrast, Henry IV and Hal are in firm control of their appetite. This augurs well for other kinds of control. In *Henry V*, Henry lists the qualities of the ideal Englishman. The list includes being "spare in diet" (2.2.131).

The word "diet" meaning restriction of food is a very recent coinage. In Shakespeare's day, diet meant simply the day's allowance of food, from the Latin noun *dies* (day). It also meant a day's allowance of anything—work, wages, travel—and hence came to mean a conference (something that occupied a day). Thus, the Imperial Diet of Worms (1521) was not a menu of annelids but a gathering of church and state (an important one, in which the excommunicated Martin Luther was summoned to recant his teachings). Hamlet puns on this event when, questioned about the location of the dead Polonius, he replies that the courtier is "at supper", not "where he eats but where 'a [he] is eaten: a certain convocation of politic worms are e'en at him" (4.3.17; 19–20).

When we look in the mirror we might wish, like Hamlet, that "this too too solid flesh would melt, / Thaw, and resolve itself into a dew" (1.2.129–30). But Hamlet was contemplating suicide, not cellulite. And although Costard, the clown in *Love's Labour's Lost*, fasts for a week on water and bran, this is an imposed punishment, not a detoxification diet. Shakespearean characters are more likely to suffer from overeating than undereating.

In Shakespeare, dietary excess is a metaphor for other kinds of excess. Shakespeare advises us to choose the middle way: "Be moderate, be moderate" (*Troilus and Cressida*); "love moderately" (*Romeo and Juliet*); "laugh moderately" (*Love's Labour's Lost*). Food is an emotional issue, a metonymy for emotion. In today's Western culture of indulgent overeating and obsessive undereating Shakespeare's dietary metaphors are easily accessible to us.

As we see repeatedly throughout this book, Shakespeare diagnoses many relationship problems as problems of excess: jealousy, racism, unrequited love, family or gender conflict. And problems of excess are problems of vision; excess is a failure to see things correctly. We must work hard to "see better." Easier said than done: how do we implement this advice? That is the subject of the next chapter.

# Ten

## POSITIVE THINKING

*Love looks not with the eyes but with the mind.*

—*A Midsummer Night's Dream*

Love is an act of will. It is an achievement of character, not an external event.

I am not talking about *falling* in love. Of course that happens (or can happen) like a bolt of lightning, making us feel that we have been swept away by events beyond our control. All our romantic clichés (I have already used two) illustrate this: we get *swept* off our feet, we *fall* in love, we are *hit* by lightning. Note the kinetic energy in the metaphors of speed and surprise, of helplessness and passivity. This is not an act of will; this is something that happens to us.

But the day-to-day business of loving, of maintaining a loving attitude, requires effort.

That may sound off-putting so let's put it another way: love is an act of imagination. As Shakespeare says in the play that best illustrates this, *A Midsummer Night's Dream*, "Love looks not with the eyes but with the mind" (1.1.234).

Love is an emotion that transforms. In *A Midsummer Night's*

*Dream*, Shakespeare tells us: "Things base and vile, holding no quantity [that is, shapeless] / Love can transpose to form and dignity" (1.1.232–33). When we fall in love we "transpose" (transform) instinctively because we see beyond the external. When we stop seeing this way we think we have fallen out of love. But it is not love that has failed, it is our imagination.

I have a glamorous girlfriend whose heroes have always been equivalently tall and athletic. Yet she married a spindly bookish man who was a foot shorter than she is in her stocking feet. ("It is better to have loved a short man than never to have loved a tall," says humorist Miles Kington.) But my friend saw the Hollywood hero within, and she has never stopped viewing him this way because she has never lapsed into viewing him comparatively. If you want your partner to be more *x*, less *y*, a little bit more *z*, you will always be disappointed because no one person can match your entire shopping list of looks or qualities. My friend concentrated on her husband's sparkling eyes and winning smile; she focused on his enthusiasm and generosity; and what she saw was a hero.

And if you tell someone every day that they are great, they will be.

One caveat: imagination can be used negatively as well as positively. Problems arise when one is in love with an image of how a person might be rather than how he or she is. As we saw in chapter 6, this is Helen's problem in *All's Well That Ends Well*—she loves an image not a reality. This is a problem of imagination, a problem of faulty seeing (characterized in *All's Well* by images of idolatry, worshiping a man-made image). There is a difference between imagining someone as something they are not and focusing imaginatively on what they are. The first is self-deception; the second is appreciation. The first inevitably leads to heartbreak; the second makes love stronger—or, in Shakespeare's words, it "grows to something of great constancy."

It seems that my girlfriends are all married to men who are great chefs. How I envy them! How I long to come home, enter a kitchen warm with gourmet aromas, and inquire "What's for dinner?" My husband is not adept in the kitchen. But cooking supper is simply one way of caring for another person, so my imagination must attend to other manifestations of spousal care. He brings me tea in bed in the morning and ensures my supplies of chocolate never run out. Now that's care! And as a sous-chef and scullery maid he is superb. (Pity the assistant: guests compliment the chef, but no one ever says, "Those pots were really, *really* clean.") Rightly viewed, these activities more than equal dinner. In terms of thought and time and effort these earn him five Michelin stars.

It's too easy to focus on what someone is not. Lack is always visible whereas what is present we take for granted. We ignore it; we don't see it. We have to make an effort to see it. We have to use our imagination to make it ever present. Seeing is not a passive activity, technical reception of an optical image. It is a choice, a skill. It is something about which we need to be reminded, something in which we need to be instructed, like Lear: "see better." Love is about seeing better, viewing imaginatively.

We tend to think of imagination as creating something that doesn't exist. Imagination in Shakespeare is not a synonym for make-believe; it is a synonym for seeing something creatively. When Helen in *All's Well* says that her "imagination / Carries no favor [face] in't but Bertram's" she does not mean that she is fabricating a picture of Bertram. She means that her impressionable mind can think of no one else. Hermia's father says something similar about his daughter in *A Midsummer Night's Dream*. He accuses Lysander of having "stol'n the impression of [Hermia's] fancy" (1.1.32): Lysander has wooed Hermia, created a good image, made her fall in love with him. He has altered her imagination, how she sees things.

Whether one calls this creative visualization (as do spiritual writers) or cognitive restructuring (as do behavioral psychologists) or the power of positive thinking (as does Norman Vincent Peale) or imagination (as does Shakespeare), it is the same principle. Changing how we see things actually changes reality. We can create our own happiness; we can make love happen.

Shakespeare's great investigation of imagination is *A Midsummer Night's Dream.* The play's presiding duke is Theseus, a believer in the rational, the tangible, the visible over the imaginative. In act 5 when the four young lovers recount their confusion in love during their night in the wood, Theseus is skeptical. He dismisses their stories as "shaping fantasies" (5.1.5) and "antic [grotesque or antique] fables" (5.1.3), and he links their imagination with that of lunatics and poets: "The lunatic, the lover, and the poet / Are of imagination all compact [composed]" (5.1.7–8).

Yet this believer in the rational who is so dismissive of antique fables is no more than an antique fable himself, a creation of classical mythology. We have as much evidence for Theseus's existence as we do for the lovers' experience. To dismiss one is to dismiss both. Furthermore, Theseus has already demonstrated the ways in which imagination can see more than is in front of your eyes. Recalling the tours in which his royal presence reduced eloquent subjects to nervous stuttering and silence, he says: "out of this silence yet I pick'd a welcome" (5.1.100). In other words, he was able to see what was not there. His imaginative vision created a welcome from silence. Theseus believes in the power of imagination even though he says he does not. Or rather, he believes in it in the realm of performance but doesn't see its relevance to the world of love.

*A Midsummer Night's Dream* constantly explores the traffic between imagination and reality, between the relation of things seen and things thought. Act 1 introduces the world of love. Hermia laments that her father, Egeus, does not see things from her point of view: "I would my father look'd but with *my* eyes." Theseus admonishes her, "Rather your eyes must with *his* judgment look" (1.1.56–57; my italics). In other words, the daughter must obediently see things from her father's point of view.

But her father's vision is not demonstrably correct or even remotely justifiable. Egeus wants Hermia to marry Demetrius. Demetrius is from the same background as Hermia's chosen beloved, Lysander; Demetrius is as rich as Lysander and as good-looking as Lysander. Hermia can therefore have no logical reason for preferring Lysander. And that's the point: love sees things differently. It is based on imagination, not reason.

If Hermia, faced with two equal men, sees one differently from the other, so does Demetrius when faced with two equal women. He loves Hermia in preference to Helena, despite the fact that the women are considered equally beautiful, despite the fact that Helena loves him, and despite the fact that he previously loved Helena. Helena laments:

> Through Athens I am thought as fair as she.
> But what of that? Demetrius thinks not so;
> He will not know what all but he do know. (1.1.227–29)

The rational vocabulary—"thinks," "knows"—is misleading. It is a question of opinion, of vision, of how you see things. But vocabulary of reason is the only vocabulary humans have for non-rational phenomena: love, imagination.

During their night in the wood outside Athens, the lovers experience the dark, nightmarish world of the imagination. Puck's mistake with the magic love juice, whose magical property is to make either "man or woman madly dote / Upon the next live creature that it sees" (2.1.171–72), means that Lysander rejects Hermia in favor of Helena. The juice also redirects Demetrius's love to Helena, but instead of being thrilled by this desired change of affection, Helena views the double adoration as humiliating mockery. She further concludes that Hermia is complicit in the plot: "Now I perceive, they have conjoin'd all three, / To fashion this false sport, in spite of me" (3.2.193–94). Helena runs away from her three Athenian companions and trudges through the dark, muddy wood alone; the two men abandon Hermia and fight each other over Helena. Chaos reigns, until the mistake is reversed by a second magic herb.

But something odd has happened. The second magic herb returns Lysander's love to Hermia. Fine: that is the situation we were in at the start of the play. But Demetrius's love has been redirected to Helena—the situation *before* the play began. (One of the accusations Lysander makes against Demetrius in act 1 is that he has loved and abandoned Helena). So although act 5 returns Lysander to normality, it returns Demetrius to a *prior* reality. What guarantee do we have that Demetrius's love will not alter again as it has done before?

This has troubled critics. So too has the means by which the plot is resolved: a magic love juice, externally applied. Floral eyedrops, applied by fairies! This is hardly the introspective self-reflection that leads to self-correction in all other Shakespeare comedies. (Think, for example, of Beatrice's anguished acknowledgment in *Much Ado About Nothing* that she has been proud and disdainful.) The lifestyle advice of the kind we have come to expect from Shakespeare here seems remote given that we do not have access to magic potions.

But, in fact we do. The love juice comes from the pansy. This source is explained and underlined in the play: Oberon takes over fourteen lines to tell us its history. Etymologically the word pansy ("paunsy" in one Elizabethan spelling) comes from the French *pensée*, which means not just "thought" as it does today but "imagination" or "vision." Demetrius thus vows to love Helena not because of an external event (the application of juice from a flower) but because of an internal event: the reordering of his vision, a change in how he sees things, *pensée*. We cannot change reality, but we can change our perception of reality. We can change how we see others and how we see ourselves. We can "see better." The magic lies within; it is the human mind. It is not the floral juice that is magic but what it represents: the power of perception. Shakespeare simply uses the pansy to stage what is otherwise unstageable, the role of imagination in love.

Changing how you see things can be difficult. In *Richard II* the king sentences Bolingbroke to exile for ten years (later reduced to six). Bolingbroke's father, John of Gaunt, tries to rouse his son from despair by encouraging him to view the banishment creatively: "Call it a travel that thou tak'st for pleasure. / . . . Think not the King did banish thee, / But thou the King. / . . . say I sent thee forth to purchase honor, / And not the King exil'd thee; or suppose, / Devouring pestilence hangs in our air, / And thou art flying to a fresher clime" (1.3.262, 279–80, 282–85). He continues with many more examples of imaginative transformation. It is quintessentially Shakespearean advice: see things differently and they will become different. But Bolingbroke resists it: "Who can hold a fire in his hand / By thinking on the frosty

Caucasus? / Or cloy the hungry edge of appetite / By bare imagination of a feast? / Or wallow naked in December snow / By thinking on fantastic summer's heat?" (1.3.294–99). He has a point. (I might add, however, that as an impecunious and hungry graduate student I often read cookbooks with color pictures at bedtime in an attempt to cloy the hungry edge of appetite; it sometimes worked.)

But it is true that imagination can have physical consequences, can affect your body chemistry. We see this most obviously in situations of fear. Last week I watched a neighbor's child climbing his ten-foot garden wall. Automatically I imagined him stumbling, falling, injuring himself. I saw these things in my mind, like a video; and the imagined event made my mouth dry, my palms clammy, and my heart race. These were *physical* reactions to an *imagined* event.

If this can happen with negative emotions such as anxiety, it stands to reason that it can happen with positive emotions. Imagining something positive—conquering an illness—should, logically, have a similar effect, flooding our system with helpful chemicals. A colleague with high blood pressure was told to imagine little men with paintbrushes swimming through his arteries, stroking away the silted-up cholesterol. Bolingbroke's counterexamples are physical and material; yet imagination can work magic on them too. And he has nothing to lose by trying.

In the lovers' plot in *A Midsummer Night's Dream* we see the creative power of imagination in love. We meet this motif again in the fairy plot. When the love juice is applied to the eyes of the fairy queen, Titania, she falls in love with Nick Bottom, the weaver who, as a result of Puck's prank, has been temporarily transformed into an ass. Titania declares undying love for Bottom. Bottom replies, wisely, "Methinks, mistress, you should have little reason for that. And yet, to say the truth, reason and love keep little company together now-a-days" (3.1.142–44). The forces that fuel love are the opposite of everything rational.

The irrational nature of love is not confined to mortal marriage. When Bottom is restored to his own identity, he remembers his metamorphosis only as a dream. He gives us a garbled account of the experience:

> I have had a dream, past the wit of man to say what dream it was . . . The eye of man hath not heard, the ear of man hath not seen, man's hand is not able to taste, his tongue to conceive, nor his heart to report, what my dream was. (4.1.205–6, 211–14)

Bottom's speech, with its misaligning of the senses, is a parody of 1 Corinthians 2:9: "The eye hath not seen, nor the ear heard, neither have entered into the heart of man, the things which God hath prepared for them that love Him." Bottom here reminds us of St. Paul, tells us that there is a love beyond human comprehension, beyond logic, beyond rational explanation. That love is divine love.

When we fall inexplicably in love with another human being, we see the divine. How you choose to interpret the divine is up to you. In Homer, the divine is equated with a change in someone's behavior. Characters know when a god has been with them (or someone else) because of the change in them. ("He felt the change and was overcome with awe for he realized a god had been with him"; "It is obvious that the gods are teaching you this bold and haughty way of speaking"; *The Odyssey*, Book I). In Shakespeare, love's irrationality is a secular version of divine experience. Love touches a part of us that is beyond daily logic. Love enables us to see beyond the material and physical, the tangible and visible. Love's irrationality is a form of magic.

Mother Teresa said that "we can do no great things, only small things with great love." Shakespeare would agree. In his plays small things becomes great things; love transforms; and it is imagination that is the enabling power.

For Shakespeare's lovers, the world of the emotions is often literally another world: the wood outside Athens in *A Midsummer Night's Dream*, the Forest of Arden in *As You Like It*, the Illyrian coast on which Viola is shipwrecked in *Twelfth Night*. Critics call this holiday environment in Shakespeare's plays the "green world" because it is so often literally a pastoral space. But the "green world" is also a metaphor: it is the emotional space where problems are solved and couples are united.

As with all holiday worlds, however, the experience is temporary: the lovers must return to court, to the city, to daily life (and the women to women's clothes!). This does not mean that they forget their experiences: they have changed and developed and must now use their new selves in the old world. After their night in the wood, the lovers in *A Midsummer Night's Dream* compare their experiences. Helena says with awe, "I have found Demetrius like a jewel" (4.1.191). Her simile refers to a stock situation in romance tales in which travelers to imaginary lands return with some tangible souvenir; this souvenir (often an item of jewelry) prevents them dismissing their experience as a dream. For Helena, her new relationship is the jewel.

We have our modern equivalent of Shakespeare's green world.

When we fall in love, we enter another world: we experience the delirious heights of reciprocated emotion, the joyous solemnity of lifelong commitment, the confident vision of future happiness. Yet the pressures and stresses of daily life can make these emotions seem as distant and unreal as any fairy world. (As someone once said: "Marriage is easy; it's the living together afterward that's difficult.") So how do we retain these magical emotions in the real world? What tokens can we bring back from our green world of courtship and commitment? What prompts can we give our imagination to help us recall the magical world and "see better" in the real world to which we have returned?

In marriage, one of my prompts is my husband's wedding ring. This prompt initially happened accidentally. Driving to work together one rushed morning, I was on the verge of being curt and critical—"Why are you always late?"—when I caught sight of the ring on my husband's hand as he changed gear. (This is Britain, remember; we change gear with the left hand.) This glimpse instantly and unexpectedly transported me back to the day I placed the ring there and the emotions that accompanied this action. Instead of feeling critical I felt overwhelmed by his courage in marrying me, by his trust in me and our future. Impossible then to criticize.

Now when I feel tempted to say something unmaritally mean, I consciously look at his ring. It never fails. The reminder of a prior occasion transforms the present, replacing petty complaint and irritation with love remembered and reenacted.

The same thing happens when couples decorate their homes with framed wedding photos and holiday pictures, or when they have code words and private phrases. These are souvenirs from the magical world of love and optimism. These are tokens that cue the imagination.

And imagination has a physical knock-on effect. Theseus dismisses the lover's stories as imagination, but Hippolyta acknowledges that imagination "grows to something of great constancy" (5.1.26). If you see something differently, you can make it reality. And that is true not just of the initial moment of vision but all subsequent moments of recall.

# Eleven

# FORGIVENESS

*The pow'r that I have on you is to spare you; /*
*The malice towards you, to forgive you.*

—*Cymbeline*

Much of this book is devoted to discussions of love. So far I have tended to assume that the object of love is a romantic partner, or a family member, or a friend. But there is another recipient of love: oneself.

Loving oneself is much harder than loving another. Yet for relationships with others to function healthily, we need first to have a healthy, loving relationship with ourselves.

Loving oneself is not the same as self-love. Self-love is narcissism; it is what Malvolio suffers from in *Twelfth Night*. Olivia tells him, "You are sick of self-love, Malvolio, and taste with a distemp'red appetite" (1.5.90–91). Self-love requires correction: it is an illness, a faulty appetite, a wrong way of seeing.

Loving oneself means accepting oneself. And learning to accept oneself is tied up with the notion of forgiving oneself. We tend to be much harder on ourselves than on others. We don't cut ourselves the same slack. We don't tolerate the same errors or inefficiencies. We don't accept the failings we do in others; we beat ourselves up over things we would unhesitatingly forgive in others. We don't extend forgiveness to ourselves.

In *The Winter's Tale*, Leontes spends sixteen years repenting a fault and performing penance. In fact, a waiting woman tells him that he has "paid down / More penitence than done trespass." But, she continues, he has omitted one crucial thing: he has not forgiven himself. She advises him, "Do as the heavens have done, forget your evil, / With them, forgive yourself" (5.1.3–6).

Forgiving is the first step to loving. If love is about generosity, so is forgiveness, as its etymology shows: it comes from the Old English verb "to give" (*giefan*), with the prefix "for" functioning simply as an intensifier. To forgive, then, means really, *really* to give. It's the ultimate gift.

To understand forgiveness we need to look at its opposite: grievance. Grievance is about holding on to the past, about not moving on. Grievance is refusal to forget. Grievance is about withholding—withholding generosity, kindness, humanity. For Shakespeare, grievance in action is known as revenge. In *Richard III* Shakespeare places revenge and forgiveness in opposition: "If thy revengeful heart cannot forgive" (1.2.173).

Revenge can be comic and creative (and presumably temporarily satisfying). In *Twelfth Night* the comic characters seek revenge on the haughty steward, Malvolio. Feste nurses a grievance against the steward for his criticism of Feste's fooling in act 1 (he later quotes Malvolio's words back to him, making it clear that he has harbored a grudge all this time). Fabian also nurses a grievance against Malvolio because Malvolio got him into trouble with Olivia "about a bear-baiting" (2.5.8). The forged letter, which encourages Malvolio to believe Olivia is in love with him, is part of a comic conspiracy to humiliate the steward.

But the conspirators don't stop here. The next stage of their trick results in Malvolio being incarcerated in chains in a dark dungeon as a madman. Comic revenge becomes cruelty; even the conspirators acknowledge that the situation has gone too far and they wish it were over: "I would we were well rid of this knavery" (4.2.67–68).

I once heard a radio program about women who had got their own back on an unfaithful partner. One woman cut off the right sleeve of all her husband's Savile Row suits. Another raided her husband's prized wine cellar and deposited a bottle of vintage claret on the doorstep of every house in the vicinity. Comically extreme though these examples are, like the revenge on Malvolio in *Twelfth Night*, they show that grievance is never passive. It is the active infliction of harm on another (as we see from its root, the French verb *grever*, to harm.)

Forgiveness is everything grievance is not. It is about letting go, about embracing the future, about giving. Giving to others and giving to one's self. And it is also about accepting oneself. Recall that to "accept" means to "receive." If one gives to oneself, if one for-gives oneself, by definition one accepts oneself.

Like Corin in *As You Like It*. This peaceful shepherd utters a great speech of self-acceptance, refusing to be shamed by the courtly clown Touchstone. Touchstone sophistically argues that Corin's pastoral life is "damnable" because it is uncourtly and uncivilized. Corin offers an eloquent statement of who he is: "Sir, I am a true laborer: I earn that [what] I eat, get that I wear, owe no man hate, envy no man's happiness, glad of other men's good, content with my harm [am patient when things go wrong], and the greatest of my pride is to see my ewes graze and my lambs suck" (3.3.73–77). He refuses to be ashamed of his life or himself. Shame is a reaction to what other people think; Corin knows that it is what *he* thinks and feels that matters. He accepts himself, he gives to himself, he for-gives himself.

～つ

My daily paper runs a weekly problem page in which a reader's dilemma is presented, inviting solutions by other readers. A recent column caught my eye. It was not the problem that attracted my attention but one of the proposed solutions. The reader was refusing to have her elderly mother visit for Christmas. The mother had failed to protect the reader from childhood abuse so the reader now wished to sever all contact. The reader's husband and adult children did not support this idea, however. Other readers were asked for their advice.

The first letter, from another victim of abuse, struck me as so perspicaciously wise that I quote it here. The advice was simply to forgive, and the rationale was as follows:

> Forgiveness will liberate you from the cycle of abuse. This does not mean that you would be letting her off the hook, but it would free you from your pain and anger. By not forgiving her, you are giving away control over your life; take that away from her and empower yourself. Do it soon before she dies, because once she is gone it will be much harder to gain your freedom from her.

The common sense here is remarkable. (But, of course, the thing about common sense is it isn't common.) Forgiveness does not erase the past but it frees you from it. It puts you in the driving seat; it gives you control.

At the end of *The Two Gentlemen of Verona* the duke says, "I here forget all former griefs [grievances], / Cancel all grudge"

(5.4.142–43). No longer a suffering victim of wrongdoing, he becomes an active dispenser of forgiveness. And forgiveness enables the duke to see things differently. He tells the malefactor Valentine, "[I] / Plead a new state in thy unrivall'd merit" (5.4.144), that is, I am determined to see you as a deserving person—deserving of forgiveness (and, because dukes can do these things, deserving a knighthood). He's back in control.

Forgiveness is a simple theory; the practice is more difficult. And I am not the best exemplar. For me, forgiveness can sometimes be an F word, something to be avoided.

The emotions at the end of my relationship with Mr. Chide developed into grievance. Instead of letting go, I spent my time anticipating the torments my ex-boyfriend would suffer in hell. Instead of forgiving, I rehearsed the wounding retorts I would deliver when next we met. I relived bitter e-mail correspondences and tortured myself with the belated composing of perfect ripostes. All of this simply served to keep open and raw the wounds that might otherwise be given a chance to heal. I was not only sowing the seeds of bitterness but watering and lovingly tending them. My wise girlfriend-counselor said sympathetically but sternly, "You've got to wish him well. You have to pray that he finds peace." In other words: forgive him and let him go.

Shakespeare's word for letting go is "forget." Shakespeare usually uses the verb "forgive" in association with "forget." Indeed, the phrase "forgive and forget" is now a cliché. The two concepts go together: to forgive you have to forget, you have to let go. Richard II instructs his nobles, "forget, forgive, conclude and be agreed" (1.1.156). Lear asks Cordelia to "forget and forgive." In

*3 Henry VI* Queen Margaret declares, "I forgive and quite forget old faults" (3.3.200). At the end of *All's Well That Ends Well* the king overcomes his desire for revenge on Bertram: "I have forgiven and forgotten all, / Though my revenges were high bent [extremely focused] upon him" (5.3.9–10).

But forgetting and forgiving is a conscious effort (like loving in chapter 10). In the speech preceding this one in *All's Well*, Bertram's mother beseeches the king "to *make* it [Bertram's fault] / Natural rebellion, done i'th' blade of youth" (5.3.5–6; my emphasis). In other words, the king can choose whether to view Bertram as a criminal or whether to redefine ("make") Bertram's transgression as teenage rebellion. The king chooses the latter. He shuns revenge and chooses to forgive and forget. He makes the choice—and the effort—to "see better."

Some Shakespeare characters are as slow to learn how to practice forgiveness as I am. In act 5, toward the end of *The Tempest*, Prospero, the exiled duke of Milan, publicly forgives his usurping brother, Antonio: "You, brother mine, that entertain'd ambition, / Expell'd remorse and nature, whom with Sebastian / . . . Would here have kill'd your king, I do forgive thee, / Unnatural though thou art." (5.1.75–79) He repeats this sentiment a few lines later: "For you, most wicked sir, whom to call brother / Would even infect my mouth, I do forgive / Thy rankest fault—all of them" (5.1.130–32). But the forgiveness is clearly not without reservation, as the sentence structure shows. Each declaration of forgiveness is followed by a clause reminding us what there is to forgive—Antonio's unfraternal behavior ("unnatural"), his multiple faults ("all of them"). Prospero insistently reminds us of the transgressions he claims to have forgiven. Surely the gentleman doth protest too much? I think there's a lot of learning and healing still to take place.

For an example of how to embrace forgiveness we need to turn to *Cymbeline*. *Cymbeline* has approximately twenty-four plot complications to untie in the final scene. The play untangles with such dizzying and parodic speed that Imogen passes out cold and even King Cymbeline registers faintness: "Does the world go round?" (5.5.232). He is reunited with his two sons who were abducted in infancy but are now grown to manhood. He is reunited with his estranged adult daughter, Imogen. He is reunited with Imogen's husband whom he had banished, and whom Imogen herself believed dead. He learns that his second wife never loved him and plotted to kill his daughter. Imogen is reunited with her husband and with her brothers, all of whom she thought were dead. And so on . . . Although most of the onstage characters have transgressed against the king and each other in some way, motives and mistakes are not dwelt on. Imogen's husband Posthumus confronts the villain Iachimo, who traduced Imogen and led to the separation of husband and wife. Instead of nurturing hurt or vengeance, Posthumus says simply, "The pow'r that I have on you is to spare you; / The malice towards you, to forgive you" (5.5.418–19). Cymbeline follows this example with a general pardon: "Pardon's the word to all" (5.5.422).

And Shakespeare shows that forgiveness can be infectious. Cymbeline says specifically that he is following the example of Posthumus: "We'll learn our freeness [noble behavior] of a son-in-law" (5.5.421).

Forgiveness in Shakespeare is a reciprocal emotion; the verb often used of it is "exchange." At the end of *King Lear* Edgar offers his brother forgiveness: "let's exchange charity" (5.3.167). Laertes does the same at the end of *Hamlet*: "exchange forgiveness with me, noble Hamlet" (5.2.329). In *Henry VIII* the duke of Buckingham reveals why forgiveness should be reciprocal. He tells Sir Thomas Lovell, "I as free [that is, freely] forgive you / As I would be forgiven." He continues: "I forgive all. / There cannot be those numberless offenses / 'Gainst me, that I cannot take peace with" (2.1.82–85). He uses forgiveness and peace as synonyms; and extending peace to others brings peace to ourselves.

*Cymbeline*'s last three speeches stress the word "peace" (and note that the soothsayer who first introduces this peace bears the wonderfully resonant name of Philharmonus—love of harmony). The peace that *Cymbeline* celebrates in its last act is theologically charged. Cymbeline's reign began in 33 B.C.E., and the play ends in approximately 15 B.C.E. with a countdown to the birth of Jesus Christ. Thus the peace that *Cymbeline* anticipates is not just political peace between Rome and Britain but universal peace. Cymbeline's philosophy of forgiveness to all will soon become a reality through the example of Christianity.

The plays such as *Cymbeline* that Shakespeare wrote at the end of his career are mellow and optimistic. Human beings mess up; they suffer incredible pain for long periods of time, and then—they are given a second chance. One doesn't need to be Christian to appreciate this pattern. "Though the seas threaten, they are merciful," says the young prince Ferdinand in *The Tempest* (5.1.178) when he finds that his family has not been drowned in a shipwreck after all. The elements are merciful, the gods are merciful, and so too, eventually, are human beings. In the late romances it's never too late to heal old wrongs, to say you're sorry, to "forgive, forget, conclude and be agreed" (*Richard II* 1.1.156). It's never too late to begin again.

〜

Forgiveness implies an event or attitude to be forgiven: an injustice, a mistreatment, a wrong. The wrong may be perpetrated by a person; but it may have no specific or human cause—it may be part of a chain of disasters of tragedies—and this can make letting go harder. One feels victimized and has the world to blame (and forgive).

Shakespeare characters have their fair share of suffering, from humans and cosmos alike. The adventures of Pericles provide particularly good examples of emotional suffering. Pericles, prince of Tyre, journeys to Antioch to woo a princess (Tyre is in modern Lebanon and Antioch is in modern Syria). On finding that she is involved in an incestuous relationship with her father, Pericles flees, devastated. No longer safe at home in Tyre (because the king of Antioch knows Pericles has discovered his incestuous secret), he embarks on a voyage, but shipwreck drowns all his companions and possessions. However, it seems that every cloud has a silver lining: Pericles is shipwrecked in Pentapolis, in a country whose king has a beautiful unmarried daughter. Pericles woos this princess, wins her, and marries her. Marriage is the conventional end of Shakespearean comedy—and we're only in act 2! But God (or the gods—the world of *Pericles* is pagan despite its Christian overtones) has not finished with Pericles yet. Another journey, another storm at sea; Pericles's wife goes into labor prematurely and dies in childbirth. Pericles makes for the nearest land, Tarsus (in today's southern Turkey), and leaves the baby girl, Marina, in the care of the king and queen. They look after her for fourteen years until the queen becomes jealous of Marina's charms and arranges to have her killed. When Pericles hears that his daughter is dead, he is emotionally defeated. Losing a wife and child is too much for any human being to bear.

In such circumstances one instinctively asks: why? Pericles is no exception. When his wife dies, he asks the gods in anguish:

> Why do you make us love your goodly gifts
> And snatch them straight away? (3.1.23–24)

There is no answer to such a question, but Pericles' behavior is instructive. Like Job, he passively, patiently accepts his bad luck. The play stresses the word "patience": "patience good sir" (3.1.19, and again identically at line 26); "bear with patience / Such griefs as you yourself do lay upon yourself" (1.2.65–66).

David Jones, who directed *Pericles* for the BBC in 1983, summarizes the action of Pericles as the story of a guy who "gets hit over the head and he gets up and says that's fine with him and he gets hit over the head again and he gets up and says don't worry, I don't hold it against you and he gets hit over the head again . . ." We need to be patient until our luck changes.

*Pericles* is often compared with *King Lear*. Both kings suffer family disruption, are buffeted by the elements, and beg for patience to endure life's cruelties. Here is Lear: "You heavens, give me that patience, patience I need!" (2.4.271). And later, in the storm scene: "I will be the pattern of all patience" (3.2.37). In the storm scene in *Pericles* the king is counseled, "Patience, good sir, do not assist [augment] the storm" (3.1.19). Grief simply adds to grief; patience helps assuage it. In *Cymbeline* the Welsh brothers note that their new visitor, Fidele, is torn between these two emotional attitudes. "I do note / That grief and patience, rooted in them both, [Fidele's smiles and sighs] / Mingle their spurs [roots] together," says one brother, to which his sibling responds, "Grow, patience, / And let the stinking elder, grief, untwine / His perishing root with the increasing vine" (4.2.58–60). In other words, the dangerous elder tree—viewed negatively by the Elizabethans because it was the tree on which Judas was supposed to have hanged himself—is strangling the vine's growth; grief is strangling patience.

Hamlet too turns his thoughts toward a metaphorical elder tree. His grief at the loss of his father and at the remarriage of his mother prompts him toward suicide. When we first meet him he is considering putting an end to his sufferings. Why, he asks, should he "suffer / The slings and arrows of outrageous fortune" when he could easily "end them" (3.1.57–59). But for Shakespeare suicide is not the answer to suffering. Patience is. Throughout the canon characters seek, or are advised to seek, patience. "Have patience, gentle Julia," counsels Proteus in *The Two Gentlemen of Verona*, one of Shakespeare's first plays; "I must, where is no remedy," replies Julia (2.2.1–2). "Be patient," pleads Gonzalo in *The Tempest* (1.1.15), one of Shakespeare's last plays. In fact, patience is invoked as a desideratum in *every* Shakespeare play!

Forgiveness is a specific form of patience in Shakespeare's plays; it is patience in practice. And forgiveness is also an aspect of love in Shakespeare; several plays illustrate that love is an endless act of forgiveness. In tragedies like *King Lear* forgiveness comes almost too late (father and daughter are reunited, but the political damage has been done; see chapter 2, "Family"). But in the late romances like *Cymbeline* the plays are rescued from the tragedy that suffering might cause by the timely display of unconditional magnanimity. In these plays suffering is healed by forgiveness.

$\sim$

As I write this I am listening to a radio interview with three families who have lost a loved one to violence—racist attack, terrorism, and teenage mayhem. One of the mothers has made a statement of forgiveness to her son's killers: "I forgive them. What happened is between them and God." But another says, "I can never forgive. They don't deserve forgiveness."

For Shakespeare, the question isn't whether others deserve our forgiveness. No one made us a judge of that. (As Sir Thomas Browne wrote in *Religio Medici*, "No man can justly censure or condemn another, because indeed no man truly knows another.") The question is whether our own nature is fine enough to prefer generosity over grievance.

But if you still prefer grievance, forgive anyway as it may, paradoxically, satisfy your desire for vengeance. Oscar Wilde explains: "Always forgive your enemies. Nothing annoys them so much."

∽

The wonderful thing about forgiveness is that it carries no risks. Most emotions or interactions with other human beings, whether positive or negative, are a risk (love carries the risk of loss, hatred runs the risk of retaliation). But there is no negative comeback to forgiveness. Even if someone refuses to accept your forgiveness, it damages them, not you.

The word "risk" appears nowhere in Shakespeare. It didn't exist in his day (it's a late-seventeenth-century coinage, imported from French). However, the *concept* of risk—venture, hazard—is everywhere. Forgiveness is a good preparatory topic for risk—if you can forgive, you are more able to take risks. And in Shakespeare's plays risk is a concept particularly associated with marriage. Let's move on to the twin subjects of love and risk.

# Twelve

## TAKING RISKS

*Who chooseth me must give and hazard all he hath.*

—*The Merchant of Venice*

My husband and I met in our forties and married less than nine months after first meeting. (When he proposed to me in a restaurant on bended knee I thought he had dropped his napkin.) In the weeks before the wedding, I was nervous. And if I was nervous, my husband was terrified. Byron's statement in 1814 aptly described his state: "I am about to be married—and am of course in all the misery of a man in pursuit of happiness." The priest who married us, a close friend, knew of our nerves and in his wedding address reminded us of the risk we were taking. "Why are they here?" he asked the congregation dramatically, rhetorically. "Two people who have shown that single life *works*. Why give it up? Why take the risk?"

The concept of risk was reinforced by the poetic presence of John Milton in our wedding ceremony. Suddenly the extracts we had chosen from *Paradise Lost* represented not the lyrical poetry of marriage but the risk chronicled in the rest of the poem, the risk when your life is incorporated with that of another. Milton's

Adam falls because his life, his fate is inseparable from Eve's. She eats the apple, and he follows because "our state cannot be severed, we are one. / One flesh; to lose thee were to lose myself."

Risk is a highly appropriate metaphor for all relationships, for the way humans make emotional investments without guarantee of gain or even expectation of return. And it is a particularly apt metaphor for love. In the week before our wedding my husband and I were discussing our nerves with our priest and he asked us how were dealing with them. "Well," said my husband in mild bemusement, "I've been getting lectures on *The Merchant of Venice* . . ."

*The Merchant of Venice* is a play about love. It is also a play about risk. The two, as Shakespeare shows, are one and the same.

The merchant of the play's title, Antonio, is a wealthy businessman with ships and merchandise all over the globe. So wealthy is he that he can afford to be generous; consequently, he lends money without charging interest. His friend, Bassanio, is at the other end of the financial scale. His impecuniosity is not due to bad luck but to bad habits: he confesses, "I have disabled mine estate, / By something showing a more swelling port / Than my faint means would grant continuance" (1.1.123–25). As Errol Flynn said, his problem lies in reconciling his gross habits with his net income.

When the play opens, Bassanio is borrowing money from Antonio to finance a love venture: he wishes to travel to Belmont to win the hand of the rich lady Portia. This is not the first time that Bassanio has borrowed from Antonio. In fact, Bassanio cheerfully admits that he is a bad risk, having lost all the money that Antonio has lent him on previous occasions. He justifies his new request for funds with a sporting analogy: shooting another arrow after a lost arrow often enables you to retrieve both. Antonio lends Bassanio the money, not because it is a potentially profitable venture (it cannot be since Antonio does not exact interest), nor because it will be a reliable return of capital (Bassanio's track record is disastrous), but because he loves his friend.

Bassanio's initial motive in wooing Portia, like that of many Shakespearean wooers, is financial. But the financial imagery in *The Merchant of Venice* has more to it than simple gain. It is mythological: Bassanio is a second Jason in search of the Golden Fleece.

Jason was a legendary Greek hero who had been told that he could inherit his kingdom (which his half-brother had taken) in exchange for the Golden Fleece of a magical ram, sacred to Zeus. Jason succeeds in this quest after many sea journeys, trials, and adventures. The imagery of Bassanio as a second Jason is thus an image of adventure rather than greed. The money is not the point. The mercantile imagery simply expresses, in language we all understand, what love is: a venture, an adventure, a hazard, a risk. We invest ourselves emotionally. And as with all investments, we may wreck ourselves or we may find ourselves enriched beyond measure.

There is no such thing as a safe investment. As the British economist Lord Bauer explained in a more recent context, "A safe investment is an investment whose dangers are not at that moment apparent."

When Bassanio arrives in Belmont he undergoes a love test designed by Portia's dead father. He has to choose one of three caskets—gold, silver, or lead. If he finds Portia's portrait in his chosen casket, he can claim Portia as his bride. Undistracted by the gold and silver caskets and their suggestion of riches and merit, Bassanio selects the humble lead casket. The lead casket—the winning casket—bears the motto, "Who chooseth me must give and hazard all he hath" (2.7.9). This cryptic motto, Bassanio realizes, provides a daunting but realistic definition of love and marriage.

In Shakespeare's day the word "venture" had not yet split off from "adventure." Thus meanings that are for us distinct, overlapped. In 1615, Alexander Niccoles, a writer on marriage, explained in his *Discourse of Marriage and Wiving:* "Marriage is an adventure [exciting undertaking], for whosoever marries, adventures; he adventures [risks] his peace, his freedom, his liberty, his body." (And, we might add, *her* peace, *her* freedom, *her* liberty, *her* body.)

Gloria Steinem cynically commented that "women's total instinct for gambling is satisfied by marriage." Shakespeare makes the same observation, but for him it is neither gender specific nor cynical. Marriage is a venture in which we give all we have and risk all we have. Love, like friendship, does not operate a profit and loss account. Paradoxically, however, if we give and hazard all we have, the gains can be immeasurable.

This is a concept of love we have lost in today's risk-averse world. Prenuptial agreements are common; you can even take out insurance policies against your marriage failing! Portia has the opposite attitude—she gives everything she has to Bassanio. And everything she has is not her investment portfolio but herself: "One half of me is yours, the other half—yours—" Note how the intellectual penny drops as she is speaking. We see her change of thought in the structure of her sentence. She starts to say that because she is now 50 percent Bassanio's, she is only 50 percent her own; "One half of me is yours, the other half mine" is what she intends to say. But she realizes that this is not correct. The repetition of "yours" clearly comes as a surprise to her, and so she has to provide an explanation: "One half of me is yours, the other half—*yours*— Mine own, I

would say; but if mine, then yours, / And so all yours"
(3.1.16–18; my emphasis).

I first thought of *The Merchant of Venice* as a play about nuptial risk just before I got married. I'm good at loyalty but bad at commitment. (Loyalty is *voluntary* commitment; consequently it doesn't alarm me because I feel in control.) For me, a restaurant booking represents a terrifying commitment; so do all timetabled events, even if I'm looking forward to them. I am completely phobic about flying. (I agree with Mel Brooks: "If God had intended us to fly, He would have sent us tickets.") My fear of flying is not because of any dread of disaster but because of claustrophobic incarceration. Claustrophobia is simply a fear of spatial commitment. I like aisle seats at the theater for the same reason—I want to feel I can *get out.*

You can imagine that if this is how I feel about time and space, it is also how I feel about emotions. I need to know there's an exit route. And marriage takes away your options big-time. You can't get out. (In today's culture, of course, you can legally, but it is not as simple as leaving the theater. You can't just exit emotionally.)

You can be sedated for flights, cancel theater tickets, renege on restaurant bookings, but there's no equivalent cancellation procedures for emotions. For Shakespeare, love is an unsecured investment; that is both its terror and its joy. Shakespeare acknowledges that those who love always risk loss (in whatever form: rejection, separation, death). This is the risk we take when we love; but it is not a reason not to love.

∽

What applies to romance also applies to commerce. ("Venture" in Shakespeare is repeatedly associated with merchants.) Books of business advice repeatedly remind us that you have more to lose by *not* doing things: the biggest risk you take is not taking a risk. The same is true of sports success: Olympic golds are not won by playing safe. It is no coincidence that the phrase "to go for gold" means to pull out all the stops, to venture everything. In Shakespeare "venture" is often coupled with the adverbs "madly" and "bravely," with daring and courage. Studies show that people who accept risk in life feel more fulfilled; this is because their present position (whether emotional, financial, or professional) is the result of choice, not stasis. And choice makes you feel in control. It's a lovely paradox, one of which Shakespeare would have approved: taking a risk gives you control, emotionally, even if the risk doesn't pay off. But not taking a risk leads to regret.

Author and therapist Robin Norwood has said that in relationships we share not only what we don't know about each other but what we don't know about ourselves. Cultivating oneself involves taking risks. (As Norwood explains, family and friends want you to stay the same so they can stay the same!) Her vocabulary here is Shakespeare's vocabulary in *The Merchant of Venice*. All emotional growth is a risk. You can buy travel insurance for any journey—except that of the heart.

I began this chapter with a discussion of marriage as a risk. Writers have a love-hate relationship with the subject of love and marriage. It's the source of acerbic witticisms: "One should always be in love. That is the reason one should not marry" (Oscar Wilde). It's the source of misogynist aphorisms: "a bachelor is a fellow who never made the same mistake once" (Gary Cooper in *North West Mounted Police*). Memorable one-liners on the trials and tribulations of marriage abound. Asked if she had contemplated divorce during her long marriage, English actress

Dame Sybil Thorndike quipped, "Divorce? Never. But murder often!" In the nineteenth century *Punch*'s most famous and most quoted joke was simply a heading: "Advice to Persons About to Marry: Don't."

And yet, despite this advice, we do. Despite the divorce statistics, despite cautionary antimarriage one-liners, we take the risk. The most popular story in life and literature is The Marriage Plot. Think Jane Austen; think Harlequin romance; think Hollywood film. Twenty-three of Shakespeare's plays move toward a conclusion in marriage, or contain wooings and weddings. *As You Like It* concludes with no fewer than four couples tying the nuptial knot, a mass movement to marriage, which Jacques notes satirically: "there is sure another flood toward, and these couples are coming to the ark" (5.4.35–36).

For Shakespeare marriage is not just a legal contract between a man and a woman. It is a metaphor for all human relationships. It includes friendship, strong emotional bonds of a nonsexual kind, and same-sex erotic relationships. It encompasses the relationship between the governor and the governed and it encompasses the emotional contracts between equals. In *Coriolanus* the Volscian hero Tullus Aufidius expresses his adoration for Coriolanus in a marital image. In *The Two Noble Kinsmen* the princes Palamon and Arcite discuss their friendship in similar terms. In the sonnets marriage is a metaphor for intellectual intimacy: "the marriage of true minds" (sonnet 116). Thus marriage in Shakespeare means more than a heterosexual institution. It provides a metaphor for how two people relate, how they grow to trust each other, how communities of two flourish and strengthen and increase (into families or societies). It encompasses all emotional loyalties and commitments. It provides a shorthand for any personal relationship and the risk it involves.

Thus, this chapter (like all of Shakespeare's romantic plays) is equally relevant to those who have not tied the nuptial knot and have no intention of doing so. In 1885 the reverend E. J. Hardy, an Irish army chaplain, wrote a book called *How to Be Happy Though Married*. Authors often use "happy" and "married" as oppositional terms. Philip Larkin thought "happy marriage" was an oxymoron ("like 'young poet'"). Hardy's title strikes me as an excellent subtitle for most Shakespeare plays. For Shakespeare, the reverend Hardy's "how to be happy though married" means "how to be happy though human." It is the aim of all our stories, no matter how different or how single we are.

There is no risk-free route to this destination. We take a risk when we speak out: "I myself have ventured / To speak my mind" (*Henry VIII* 5.1.40). We take a risk when we confront fear: "I am afraid and yet I'll venture it" (*King John* 4.3.5). We take a risk when we learn a new sport: "ventured / Like little wanton boys that swim on bladders [flotation devices]" (*Henry VIII* 3.2.358). All human activity is a risk.

If marriage seemed a risk to Peter and me, getting married in middle age was an even greater risk: one has more to give up, more to venture. Let's turn to the subject of what maturity means in Shakespeare's plays.

# Thirteen

# MATURITY

*Thou and I are too wise to woo peaceably.*

—*Much Ado About Nothing*

"Love is like the measles," said the Victorian dramatist Douglas Jerrold: "all the worse when it comes late in life." There is a difference between "mature love" and "mature" love. "Mature love" is the opposite of teenage infatuation. "Mature" love, on the other hand, is when teenage infatuation is felt and experienced by people who are not teenagers. I want to begin this chapter by looking at what happens when you catch emotional measles in maturity, when you experience young love late in life. This subject involves the related topic of what "mature love" does to one's lifestyle and one's career.

Today women and men are as likely to marry in their thirties and forties as in their twenties. Gone are the days when women donned their white caps at thirty, as did Jane Austen in 1805, to signal that they were off the marriage market, their age having rendered them ineligible. Surveys today of those who marry in their forties reveal interesting patterns of behavior and attitude (as compared with those who date in their forties but don't marry). Most of those who marry after forty have an active social life, particularly in sports activities; most of the women have a circle of male friends from work; most identify kindness as the quality that attracted them to their partner (over good looks); most are verbally up-front about their affection for the other, not relying on the hints that suffice for people in their twenties and thirties; and most important, most act much younger than they are. They have fun, they have romantic fun, they do fun things.

This summary comes from John T. Molloy's chapter on "Marrying After Forty" in his book *Why Men Marry Some Women and Not Others*. I hadn't read it when I met my husband, for the simple reason that, despite having spent forty years on this planet, I was not looking for someone to marry; thus Molloy's book and others like it had no appeal. In fact when I realized I was falling in love with the man who would become my husband I viewed the new emotion as a big inconvenience. It changed everything! Theater trips and companionable getting-to-know-you dinners were all very nice, but I had a busy professional life and couldn't see how a partner could be fitted in. However, as we know from Robert Burns, "the best laid plans o' mice and men gang aft agley": Peter and I married nine months after meeting, six months after starting to date.

In retrospect both Peter and I were doing everything Molloy advises. We had a high level of "information exchange," which meant we got to know each other quickly. Younger people go on dates in clubs and cinemas where the entertainment slows the rate of conversation; maturer people tend to eat in restaurants or go for walks and so accelerate their knowledge of each other through discussion. I remember leaving a downtown restaurant with Peter late one frosty evening; our walk home took us past the window of Waterstone's bookshop where I was impressed by the fact that Peter had read every book on display. ("Ah yes," said a cynical friend when I mentioned this later. "That old tactic.

You go into your local bookstore, say, 'these are the books I have read,' and pay them to put them in the window . . .") If you know what someone reads and has read, you know a lot about them. You can't get that knowledge on the dance floor.

Renaissance literature is responsible for our erroneous view that Elizabethans married young, like the fourteen-year-old Juliet. In fact the average age of marriage for men was twenty-seven, for women twenty-four. The figures are lower for the upper classes where aristocratic men married, on average, at twenty-four, women at nineteen, and the gentry married at twenty-seven for men, twenty-two for women. Men had to be economically independent before they could think of supporting a wife, hence the higher figures.

Antony and Cleopatra are clearly not young lovers. Cleopatra is sexually experienced, having had several sexual partners. She and Antony have both been married to other people, and both have children from their previous marriages. They are highly successful professional people. She is queen of Egypt, he is a "triple pillar of the world" (that is, one of the three coalition leaders of Imperial Rome), and their professional lives necessitate a commuter relationship (Egypt-Rome!). But they are willing to risk their professional status and success for their love, and Shakespeare does not criticize them for it. (For more on love and risk, see chapter 12.)

Antony's colleagues, on the other hand, do. Philo dismisses Antony's love of Cleopatra as "dotage," and Scarus characterizes Antony as a "doting mallard" (1.1.1; 3.10.19). Dotage and doting are Shakespeare's words for false love, superficial love, infatuation (as we saw in chapter 6). In *A Midsummer Night's Dream* the fairy queen, Titania, "dotes" on an ass. In *Romeo and Juliet* Romeo "dotes" on Rosaline before he meets Juliet. In *A Midsummer*

*Night's Dream* Demetrius irrationally pursues Hermia like an "idle gaud [worthless trinket], / Which in my childhood I did dote upon" (4.1.167–68). Even Antony says, "These strong Egyptian fetters I must break, / Or lose myself in dotage" (1.2.116–17). Dotage represents the irrational, the irresponsible, and the immature.

But Antony and Cleopatra's conversation and action obviate any suggestion of mere youthful infatuation. The couple mix poignantly poetic expressions of love with affectionate badinage. In their opening four-line dialogue Cleopatra affects to doubt Antony and asks him to declare his hand: "If it be love indeed, tell me how much." (We might note, incidentally, that this is the challenge of a confident woman—no one uncertain of their partner's love would risk such a statement.) Antony's playful evasive answer is a gallant compliment: "There's beggary in the love that can be reckon'd" [that is, anyone who can measure their love doesn't have very much; thus, by implication, Antony's love is great]. Cleopatra picks up the metaphor and offers to make his arithmetical task easier: "I'll set a bourn [limit] how far to be belov'd." Antony replies that she will need to find another universe before she can find a limit to his love: "Then must thou needs find out new heaven, new earth" (1.1.14–17).

Wow! You think real people don't speak like this? As one of my colleagues says: we would if we could!

However, despite maturity and confidence, Cleopatra is vulnerable in love. She is jealous of a younger woman who has a claim on Antony and is hesitant in saying what she really feels to Antony when the lovers have to part. The speech is curious:

Courteous lord, one word:
Sir, you and I must part, but that's not it [that's not what
    I mean to say];

Sir, you and I have lov'd, but there's not it; [That's not what I
     mean to say either];
That you know well. [You already know that.] Something it is
     I would—
[There's something I want to say to you . . .]
O, my oblivion is a very Antony,
And I am all forgotten. [I've totally forgotten what I was go-
     ing to say.] (1.3.86–91)

Has she really forgotten? Or is she just too nervous to say what
she wants? Three false starts suggest the latter.

An actress cannot say these lines without some idea of what
Cleopatra wants, but hesitates to ask. Jane Lapotaire, who played
Cleopatra in the BBC film in 1981, offers the logical interpretation: Cleopatra is trying to engineer a discussion of marriage.
News has just come that Antony's wife is dead (hence his speedy
and unexpected return to Rome) but Antony "never says, 'Now I'll
marry you,' which is what any woman in a triangular situation
would hope." Cleopatra wants to have this conversation (and
commitment?) before Antony departs for Rome but despite her
apparent confidence in love, her standing in the world, and her
famed reputation for beauty she cannot broach the topic; she cannot risk rejection. "Mature" love feels, suffers, and fears just as
young love does.

When Antony later submits to a political arranged marriage
with Octavius Caesar's sister, Octavia (2.2), Cleopatra anxiously
sends a messenger to report on Octavia's beauty, her coloring,
her height. She relaxes when she hears that Octavia has a low
forehead, lacks grace in walking, is not as tall as Cleopatra. She is
far from pleased, however, to hear that her rival is thirty years
old. Not for Cleopatra the consolations of Agatha Christie
(married to an archaeologist), who commented: "An archaeolo-

gist is the best husband any woman can have—the older she gets, the more interested he is in her."

Throughout the play Antony and Cleopatra, two world rulers, live for love. They play, they tease, they feast, they drink, they make love, they talk about making love. When they are apart, Cleopatra thinks and talks about having sex with Antony. Frivolous and irresponsible? Perhaps. Reassuringly healthy? Yes. The heart does not age.

Nonetheless the encounters between Antony and Cleopatra are remarkable for their nonsexuality. The couple walk the city streets in the evening and "note / The qualities of people" (that is, they enjoy people-watching and they like strolling hand in hand; 1.1.53–54). They go fishing. (You can substitute your own sporting preference here.) They wear each other's clothes. They have dinner, they chat. They talk of pleasure and of living for the moment, but the pleasures portrayed seem domestic and innocent rather than hedonistic and reprehensible. This is one of the joys of "mature" love: it can incorporate romance and routine, the delirious and the daily. (Or as my husband puts it: you can have sex and still floss your teeth.)

I said that these activities are notable for their nonsexuality. But they are nonetheless potentially sexual. Swapping clothes, for instance. Sex is clearly a destination for Antony and Cleopatra; it's just not the *immediate* destination. For them, fishing is foreplay (and dining, talking, walking . . .). And what is delightful is how much time they spend in this activity. They are not young people in a hurry.

Antony concludes that "kingdoms are clay" and "the nobleness of life / Is to do thus" (where "thus" refers to kissing Cleopatra; 1.1.35, 36–37). To onlookers this can only be dotage. After all, Antony spends his time in Egypt instead of Rome. Although everyone appreciates Cleopatra's innumerable attractions, it is hard for them to believe that love might be more important to Antony than politics, that personal life might be more important to Cleopatra than career.

In the end, however, Antony loses a sea battle because he is ruled by his heart rather than his judgment, and commands his ship to follow Cleopatra's. With this naval loss comes loss of professional dignity; he therefore takes his life. Cleopatra falls captive to Rome and also commits suicide. Both Antony and Cleopatra lose their power and prominence on the world stage. For what? For love. *All for Love* is the title of John Dryden's seventeenth-century adaptation of Shakespeare's play, a title that could have either critical or complimentary implications, although he, like Shakespeare, views the world well lost for love. In presenting the intoxicating and reckless love of this couple, a love that risked much professionally, Shakespeare forces us to reassess our priorities. Perhaps they gained more than they lost, Shakespeare says; perhaps what they lost was worth losing.

Easy to say, of course (despite my hesitant "perhaps"). Maybe the reason so many forty-somethings are quitting the rat race is that putting personal life above career is less difficult when you have already achieved. Midlife rejection of one's career stress in exchange for domestic bliss (what we call "spending more time with the family" or, more piously, "having the right priorities") does not suffer from wistful musings about the path not taken. It's possible to have it all—just not all at once.

Antony and Cleopatra's story resonates today with anyone who has tried to balance professional and personal life. This seems to be a particularly female predicament—as Gloria Steinem points out, we "have yet to hear a man ask for advice on how to combine marriage and a career." Men tend simply to add a woman to their professional life whereas women more often adapt their professional life for a man. Nonetheless I recall vividly the audience's shock and sympathy in relation to Antony's predicament at the last Royal Shakespeare Company production of the play. Antony had "gone native" with an Egyptian costume of open-toed sandals and flowing white robes. The contrast with the Romans' sculpted leather and precise belts caused sharp intakes of breath and underlined Antony's choice of priority: these were sartorial representations of a lifestyle. The Roman costumes were constrained and controlled, the Egyptian relaxed and unfettered. Antony's choice was represented as, and interpreted by the Romans as, neglect.

In one sense this is partly true—if you are a triple pillar of the world, you jeopardize an entire political structure by removing your presence and commitment, as the architectural metaphor (Shakespeare's "pillar," my "structure") makes clear. But in another sense Antony's choice is a form of bravery, every bit as heroic as his famous survival in battle with horse urine as his only source of fluid.

Giving up or reducing one's professional involvement is difficult (as we saw in chapter 2 in the case of Lear). Neither Antony nor Cleopatra is ultimately successful in the attempt— their suicides are related to professional political concerns—but part of the problem is that their culture, like ours, does not have a vocabulary to describe what they are trying to achieve. Their prioritizing of personal life is viewed as dotage, irresponsibility, abandonment of priority, loss, lack, a falling off. But while the play concludes with political loss, it also shows personal gain.

*Much Ado About Nothing* is less precise than *Antony and Cleopatra* about the ages of its protagonists, Beatrice and Benedick. They are lovers who are old enough to have loved and lost (each other) in a story that took place before Shakespeare's play begins.

Shakespeare never gives us the details of their earlier liaison. Beatrice refers to it briefly but bitterly in a cryptic comment: Benedick lent her his heart "awhile, and I gave him use [interest] for it, a double heart for his single one . . . he won it of me with false dice" (2.1.278–80). All we know of the current situation is that Beatrice and Benedick have a love-hate relationship conducted through a "merry war of words," and that their battle of wits is a good spectator/auditor sport for all around them.

Beatrice and Benedick talk a great deal about each other, and although their comments are consistently negative and critical, it is clear that anyone so preoccupied with another is far from indifferent to that other. If Shakespeare were writing this play today, he'd call it *Eternal Sunshine of the Spotless Mind.* The point is that you can't erase memories; there are some people we will always be attracted to.

The play's events—with a little creative help from the couple's friends and family—prove this observation to be valid, and Beatrice and Benedick marry in the last act even as they are still protesting and threatening to call the whole thing off. "Thou and I are too wise to woo peaceably," says Benedick (5.2.72). What does he mean by wisdom in this context? That they are experienced enough to know that romance is not an easy ride?

Throughout the years fashions have changed in the preferred ages for Beatrice and Benedick and Antony and Cleopatra. In the 2002 Royal Shakespeare Company production of *Much Ado* the fifty-year-old Harriet Walter played Beatrice, and Nicholas Le Provost, several years older, played Benedick. Benedick's rhetorical question, "Shall I never see a bachelor of threescore again?" (1.1.199–200) was a direct reference to himself and to the fact that his contemporaries were coupled. In the same season Antony and Cleopatra were played by Sinéad Cusack (aged fifty-four) and Richard Johnson (aged fifty-six), the latter with a grizzled beard, the former lithe and athletic but sensible rather than sexy. More than two decades ago, in 1982, I saw a thirty-seven-year-old Helen Mirren play Cleopatra and in 1986 I first saw Timothy Dalton on stage, playing Antony at the age of forty. In fact when Albert Broccoli saw Dalton in this role he signed him up as the next James Bond. Does current casting reflect current definitions of middle age and "mature" love?

The age at which we become middle-aged or "old" has moved upward, perhaps because we are living longer, or perhaps because we are physically active at ages when previous eras opted for matronly or patriarchal desuetude. Twenty percent of people over seventy-five say they are "middle-aged" (contrast this with an Elizabethan manuscript I once read that described a twenty-two-year-old woman as of "middle years"!). Turning sixty, Woody Allen said, "Practically a third of my life is over." Middle and old age are best epitomized in attitudes and abilities, not numbers. "Middle age occurs when you are too young to take up golf and too old to rush up to the net" (Franklin P. Adams). "Middle age is when your broad mind and narrow waist begin to change places" (E. Joseph Crossman). After a summer of osteopath visits, a friend gave me a tea towel that proclaimed, "Middle age is when your back goes out more often than you do." And whatever old age is, it is always older than we are.

In terms of romance, our society is moving more and more to the Antony and Cleopatra model. We practice serial monogamy and therefore meet our till-death-us-do-part partner after a "starter marriage"; or we marry later in life, if at all; we retire earlier; according to a recent survey the over fifties are more sexually active than they were in their twenties, liberated from the exhaustion of career or family development; older women are considered sexually attractive not just to their contemporaries but to younger men.

In *Antony and Cleopatra* Shakespeare says: age does not protect you from love, but love protects you from age. (Jeanne Moreau actually said that but Shakespeare anticipates the sentiment.)

~)

So far I have been talking about maturity in chronological terms, related to age. In *Love's Labour's Lost* Shakespeare presents maturity (and immaturity) in relation to wisdom and understanding. *Love's Labour's Lost* is a play about emotional intelligence. In this play four men woo four women, only to find themselves outwitted. The women, more emotionally mature than the men, see through their suitors at every stage.

The play opens with the king of Navarre and his three friends vowing to devote themselves to study for a period of three years. They will fast, read books, sleep only three hours a night, and forswear the company of women. It sounds a lot like university—indeed the king refers to his court as "a little academe" (1.1.13).

Shakespeare was healthily skeptical about ascetic modes of study. In *The Taming of the Shrew* the servant Tranio cautions his master, who has come to Pisa to study:

> Let's be no Stoics nor no stocks [blocks of wood and hence
> incapable of feeling], I pray,
> Or so devote to Aristotle's checks
> As Ovid be an outcast quite abjur'd. (1.1.31–33)

Love (as represented by the Roman love poet, Ovid) is important, he explains, because "no profit grows where is no pleasure ta'en" (1.1.39). Life contributes to learning; they are not opposed categories.

The king of Navarre could benefit from Tranio's advice. Navarre's vows are impractical—and not just because book learning isolated from emotional life is impractical. It turns out that the French princess and her ladies are scheduled to visit Navarre's court. They must be entertained. And so the men break the first of their idealistic vows.

In fact, in meeting, loving, and debating with the French ladies the men learn things they could not get from books. If the purpose of study is, as the king says, "that to know which else we should not know" (1.1.56), it is obvious that life and empirical experience are as educative as books. (Remember that Shakespeare himself did not attend university.) The lords will later conclude that women are "the books, the arts, the academes / That show, contain, and nourish all the world" (4.3.349–50), but at the moment they shun life for study, not realizing that the two are not exclusive.

Throughout the play the men are portrayed as charming but immature, unable to see through surface appearance. We see this most obviously in their language, which is always a peacock display, designed to dazzle. But speech must have meaning and constancy (like love) and not simply be rhetorical ornament. The men's cavalier attitude to words is seen in the ease with which they break the vow they make at the beginning of the play.

Consequently the women do not take the men's later declarations of love seriously. How can they have confidence in their wooers' speech when the men themselves are fickle in their attitudes to the things speech represents? If a word is a sign for a thing, the women expose the men's inadequacy by showing them their inability to see beyond signs to the thing/person/idea they represent. The women exchange the presents the men have given them (pearls, diamonds) and wear masks when they next receive their suitors. As a result, the men woo the wrong women. When their mistake is revealed, they realize that "we / Following the signs, woo'd but the sign of she" (5.2.468–69). In language and in love the men are misled by externals.

The men promise to give up fancy rhetoric. Berowne says he will no longer woo in rhyme, with prepared speeches, with words used as ornament, with "taffeta phrases, silken terms precise, / Three pil'd hyperboles [like very deep velvet], spruce affection [affectation], / Figures pedantical" (5.2.406–8). His textile images are all of extravagantly rich fabrics: silk, velvet, taffeta (this last could retail at 15s. [75p] a yard; compare a loaf of bread at 1d. [1/2p], or a craftsman's weekly wage of 5s. [25p]). But old habits die hard. Berowne uses affected speech to forswear affected speech when he declares that his love for Rosaline is "sans [without] flaw." Rosaline instantly exposes the affectation: "Sans 'sans' I pray you" (5.2.416). The men still have a long way to go.

The women realize this and at the end of the play impose tasks on the men to help them grow up. Although the men propose marriage, the ladies decline, because, naturally, they have viewed the men's wooing as just another example of rhetorical insincerity. They agree to meet the men again in a year to discuss love, but, as Berowne observes, "that's too long for a play" (5.2.878). (Perhaps Shakespeare should have called this play *A Very Long Engagement*.)

Q: "What's the difference between a man and a bottle of wine?" A: "A bottle of wine matures as it ages." This was the caption on a birthday card someone sent me a few years ago. It's not that Shakespearean men don't mature as they age; it's just that they don't mature as fast as women (at least in the comedies). Variants of the greeting-card message abound, all of them contrasting youth and maturity. "You're only young once but you can be immature indefinitely," says British comedian and journalist Victor Lewis-Smith. "Age is a very high price to pay for maturity," says Tom Stoppard. The lords and ladies in *Love's Labour's Lost* are indeed all young but it is only the men who are immature. The women do not confuse life and play, do not avoid the real world, do not believe that the answers are in books (or not only in books).

Let us return to the opening dialogue between the king and Berowne. Berowne asks, "What is the end [aim] of study?" (a question that every student and academic no doubt asks themselves as they embark on a life of deprivation). The king's definition is: "that to know which else we would not know" (1.1.56). I've already said above that the place to look for answers is not just books but life. But we can now be even more specific than that. "That to know which else we should not know" is forbidden knowledge; and the first forbidden knowledge is sex.

In act 5 Berowne says, "From women's eyes this doctrine I derive: / They sparkle still the right Promethean fire" (4.3.347–48). The reference to Prometheus is a reference to forbidden knowledge (Prometheus stole fire from the gods to give to mankind). The men realize now how much they can learn from women. Personal relations are a form of knowledge. You will learn more from interacting with your fellow human beings than you will from isolated book reading.

You can be young and in love in middle age, like Antony and Cleopatra. You can be young and foolish like the lords in *Love's Labour's Lost*. And you can be wise and mature in youth, like the princess of France and her ladies. Age is an attitude; age is about how you see things.

~

Goethe said, "If youth is a fault, it is one soon corrected." Shakespeare usually shows this process of correction: Beatrice's anguished realization, for example, that she is "condemn'd for pride and scorn" (*Much Ado About Nothing* 3.1.108). But in *Love's Labour's Lost* we are not allowed to see the men's maturation. For five acts they have been blind and immature. Now they are ready to grow up but we have to take it on trust: they are at the beginning of their education, but we are at the end of the play.

Shakespeare showed unusual generic daring in denying his audience a happy ending. (The stress is surely on the last word of the title: *Love's Labour's Lost*.) He is equally daring in introducing death into the last moments of a comedy. The atmosphere changes abruptly when news comes of the death of the king of France; the princess breaks off romantic play with the lords to assume her regal responsibilities in the real world. Shakespeare thus shows us two kinds of loss: romantic hopes dashed and death. Loss, and the problem of life's romantic and physical ends, is the subject of the next chapter.

# fourteen

## LOSS

*This world's a city full of straying streets,*
*And death's the market-place where each one meets.*

—*The Two Noble Kinsmen*

In chapter 9 we looked at jealousy as anticipation of loss. In this chapter I want to examine what happens when loss is not just a prospect but a reality, no longer a distant possibility but a past event. How do we cope when we have lost someone we love? There are many kinds of loss but I want to start with the most familiar: death.

The key Shakespeare play about death is *Hamlet*. In Tom Stoppard's version, *Rosencrantz and Guildenstern Are Dead*, Hamlet's friend, Rosencrantz, rehearses (un)subtle ways of probing his old schoolmate: "To sum up, your father, whom you love, dies, you are his heir, you come back to find that hardly was the corpse cold before his younger brother popped onto his throne and into his sheets, thereby offending both legal and natural practice. Now why exactly are you behaving in this extraordinary manner?"

But usurpation and incest are only adjuncts to the problem

Hamlet is trying to cope with when the play opens—the death of his father. Author and humorist Tom Masson said that *Hamlet* is the tragedy of trying to tackle a family problem too soon after college. When we think of *Hamlet* in terms of its "family problem," we tend to think of Claudius's assassination of his brother-in-law, usurpation of his crown, and his marriage to his widowed sister-in-law, Hamlet's mother. These are the issues uppermost in Rosencrantz's mind, but his detailed list of potential problems is superfluous. The clue to his question lies in the first six words: *"your father, whom you love, dies."*

It is a cliché of Shakespeare criticism that Hamlet "delays." Having agreed to avenge his father's murder, he fails to get on with the task. He indulges in introspective reflections, hangs around at home, does not take much interest in life, suffers from what we would now call depression. I confess that I did not have much sympathy with Hamlet's ennui until my own father died in the summer of 2000. I was not a university student but a forty-year-old adult. Nonetheless, I spent months being taciturn, antisocial, preferring to stay at home, unable to get on with work.

It was only then that I realized the value of the black mourning bands that bereaved people wore on their arms during the Victorian period. The bands did not mean, "give this person sympathy"; they meant, "give this person a wide berth." A bereaved person is one who will not meet deadlines. A bereaved person is one who will decline invitations to barbecues. A bereaved person is one who will not be able to "speed to his revenge" with "wings as swift as meditation."

The Renaissance had a system of year numbering related to the monarch's reign. Thus 1509 was also 1 Henry VIII (the first year of Henry VIII's reign), 1510 was 2 Henry VIII, and so on. The dual numbering registered a change of life, of regime, of emotion. I found myself dwelling on this system when my father died. On the day of his death I wandered the streets in bewilderment, trying to take stock of the new numbering system: the first day of life without my father. The next morning I woke up on day 2 AD (After Dad). As time wore on the numbering system became weeks, then months; now it is the years that I register. But one always remembers.

Hamlet is in his twenties when his father dies, and he is disabled by grief. He continues to wear his mourning clothes after the official mourning period has ended; he is antisocial and uncooperative; he resents his mother for getting on with her life (she remarries within four months); he thinks obsessively of his father; and he contemplates suicide.

Hamlet's hyperbolic descriptions of his dead father show that his attitude is typical of the early stages of grief in which the mourner idealizes the deceased. In Hamlet's opinion his father was "Hyperion" (the sun god), Jove, Mars, Mercury. Hamlet feels he "shall not look upon his like again" (1.2.188). In contrast to these divine images of perfection, Claudius, his stepfather and the new king, is a "satyr" (half man, half beast), a king of "shreds and patches" (a jester).

One might argue that Hamlet's attitude is related to the unnatural manner of King Hamlet's death: murder. (He was poisoned by "juice of cursed hebona" while he was taking an afternoon nap.) However, Shakespeare carefully presents the prince's grief as extreme, even before he finds out that his father's death was murder; Hamlet simply cannot come to terms with his loss. He objects vehemently to the fickleness of the Danish populace who once idolized Hamlet Senior but now pay extravagant sums for portraits of Claudius. His outrage here is the same as that he feels toward his mother: outrage at those who have chosen the living over the dead, the present over the past. But as Shakespeare tells us elsewhere, "Moderate lamentation is the right of the dead, excessive grief the enemy to the living" (*All's Well That Ends Well* 1.1.55–56).

~

Regardless of how we reach it, death itself is a natural phenomenon. In their first scene together, Claudius tries to console Hamlet with this reminder: "[Y]our father lost a father. / That father lost, lost his . . ." (that is, Your grandfather died. Your grandfather's father also died . . . ). The survivor must mourn (indeed, is obliged to mourn) for some time, he says, but to prolong mourning is stubborn, unspiritual, and unreasonable: "to persever / In obstinate condolement [grief] is a course / Of impious stubbornness, . . . / It shows a will most incorrect to heaven, / A heart unfortified, or mind impatient, / An understanding simple and unschool'd." The "death of fathers," he concludes, is one of the themes of life; nature says, "this must be so" (1.2.89–106.) In *The Two Noble Kinsmen* Shakespeare repeats Claudius's sentiment with a memorable spatial metaphor: "This world's a city full of straying streets, / And death's the marketplace, where each one meets" (1.5.15–16). In the less poetic but equally memorable metaphor of the TV series *Friends*, we all meet "at the checkout counter."

Claudius's philosophy comes from the school of memento mori wisdom. This Latin phrase ("remember that you have to die") describes a moral and philosophical system designed to incorporate thoughts of death into daily life. By remembering that all life ends in death and that one day you would be held accountable for your actions, you would behave morally throughout life.

Memento mori philosophy was given a material existence. Miniature skulls and skeletons were the most common memento mori items. They were incorporated decoratively in accessories such as buttons and finger rings. If you were planning to do something the church deemed immoral (for example, have sex with a prostitute), a glance at your (or her) memento mori finger ring would remind you that you would have to pay for this sin on the day of judgment. Young men often had their portraits painted with skulls; young students kept skulls on their desks. (Try substituting a skull for a diploma in today's graduation photograph and you'll get the picture, so to speak.) Artwork presented twin images (the face of a beautiful woman on one side, a skull on the other) as did funerary sculpture. At the foot of one statue in St. Paul's Cathedral is a skull, nestling discreetly in the folds of the sculpture's robes. (Punk fashion with its preference for skulls meant memento mori enjoyed an accidental revival in the 1980s. To punk I owe my collection of skull earrings, worthy of an Elizabethan.)

Whatever the artistic form—ring, button, painting, desk accessory, statue, coin—the message was the same: live life appropriately, for one day you must die. As the Book of Common Prayer has it: "In the midst of life we are in death."

The American novelist Ethel Mumford parodies the Book of Common Prayer with "In the midst of life we are in debt." What to us is parody would have been to the Elizabethans a pun. Since "th" was pronounced as "d," wordplay on death/debt was common. At the battle of Shrewsbury in *1 Henry IV* Falstaff is told to brace himself for death because it is a debt he owes: "Thou owest God a death." Protesting about premature payment, Falstaff pursues the pun: "'Tis not due yet, I would be loath to pay him before his day" (5.1.126–28). The accounting metaphor acknowledges inevitability: death is "due." Hamlet invokes the same fiscal image in the soliloquy in which he contemplates suicide. Why would anyone choose to suffer in life, he asks, when he could stab himself: "when he himself might his quietus make / With a bare bodkin [dagger]" (3.1.73–74). "Quietus est" was the formula stamped on Renaissance accounts when they had been paid (from the Latin "it is at rest"). To make your quietus, then, is to pay your account, to discharge your life's debt with death.

~

At the beginning of *Hamlet* the prince is in denial about death. His friend Horatio describes the supernatural portents surrounding the death of Julius Caesar:

> A little ere the mightiest Julius fell,
> The graves stood tenantless and the sheeted dead
> Did squeak and gibber in the Roman streets.
> . . . and the moist star . . .
> Was sick almost to doomsday with eclipse. (1.1.114–20)

These inflated images show that the young men cannot see death as other than unnatural; to them death is something that cannot take place without ghosts walking, eclipses, ominous signs.

By act 5, however, in the famous graveyard scene, we see Hamlet with a skull in his hand—a typical memento mori pose. Hamlet addresses the skull: "Get you to my lady's chamber, and tell her, let her paint an inch thick, to this favor [face] she must come" (5.1.192–94). (In other words: go and tell women that this is what a female face will look like in the grave when cosmetics will be of no help.) Hamlet now dispenses the memento mori wisdom he had earlier rejected from Claudius, reminding us that cosmetics conceal and hence deny the inevitable path toward death. His attitude to death has changed. No longer in denial about death, he can offer moral philosophy to those who are. His tone is one of quiet acceptance. In the next scene he tells the anxious Horatio: "We defy augury. There is special providence in the fall of a sparrow. If it [death] be now, 'tis not to come; if it be not to come, it will be now; if it be not now, yet it will come—the readiness is all" (5.2.219–22). Here his calm acceptance has much in common with his fellow humanist, the French essay writer Michel de Montaigne, who wrote, "I want Death to find me planting my cabbages, neither worrying about it nor the unfinished gardening."

Our contemporary culture is full of satiric references to death, designed to make us more comfortable with this taboo topic (or perhaps to disguise the fact that we are very *un*comfortable talking about this topic). A birthday card proclaims: "No one wants to be 85. Until they're 84½." And Woody Allen confessed: "I'm not afraid of dying. I just don't want to be there when it happens." Doris Day admitted that "the really frightening thing about middle age is that you know you'll grow out of it." Rolling Stones guitarist Keith Richards observes "The older you get, the older you want to get." (This strikes me as wonderfully ironic given the Stones' propensity for not aging—or, at least, not acting their age.)

Death prompts famous last lines: Voltaire, on being asked to renounce the devil, retorted, "This is no time to be making new enemies." Death is satirically considered a good career move: "Once you're dead you're made for life" (Jimi Hendrix). The classic "Dead Parrot" sketch from *Monty Python's Flying Circus* (7 December 1969) satirizes our inability to talk about death. Count the euphemisms:

It's not pining, it's passed on. This parrot is no more. It's ceased to be. It's gone to meet its maker. This is a late parrot. It's a stiff. Bereft of life it rests in peace. It would be pushing up the daisies if you hadn't nailed it to the perch. It's rung down the curtain and joined the choir invisible. It's an ex-parrot.

But although much about death has changed since the Renaissance—our reluctance to acknowledge it, the means, the pain, the location, the average age—the blunt fact of death has not. Life still ends.

Life and death were closely linked in Shakespeare's day. Neither had yet been sidelined to clinical hospital settings: both took place in the home, and often one died in the same bed in which one had been born. Old and young were cared for together in the same household. Fertility games took place in churchyards during funerals, and rosemary—the herb strewn on coffins—was also the herb for bridal bouquets. (In *Romeo and Juliet* the nurse strews Juliet's sedated body, believed dead, with the rosemary intended for her wedding that same day.) Thus, life's simultaneous capacity for ending and renewing itself was always visible.

It is often stated that the sheer familiarity of death in the Renaissance must have made death easier to cope with. The literature of the period offers no support for such a view. Ben Jonson writes poignant poems on the death of his six-month-old daughter and seven-year-old son. In Kyd's *The Spanish Tragedy* (c.1587), an atmospheric forerunner to *Hamlet*, the hero spends four acts trying to come to terms with the loss of his son; his wife, less rhetorically but no less dramatically, goes mad for grief. The death of children is clearly a premature loss; the loss of parents is not. But that does not make the loss any easier to bear, as Hamlet finds out.

The early-seventeenth-century Norwich doctor Sir Thomas Browne wrote that "The long habit of living indisposeth us for dying." He was talking about our own longevity and consequent reluctance to leave life; but his statement applies equally to others' longevity and our reluctance to lose them. When one is bereaved, people often ask, "Was it expected?" Immediately they look embarrassed as the belated recognition strikes them: expecting death does not assuage the loss.

"Heaven and earth, / Must I remember?" asks Hamlet in anguish as he contrasts the intolerable present with the idealized pre-mortem past (1.2.142–43). There are several kinds of memory. Here his memory is acute raw pain, a constant reinforcer of absence and recent loss. But although memory reinforces the void it can also fill it; memory can cause pain, but it can also console. As Constance explains in *King John*:

> Grief fills the room up of my absent child,
> Lies in his bed, walks up and down with me,
> Puts on his pretty looks, repeats his words,
> Remembers me of all his gracious parts,
> Stuffs out his vacant garments with his form;
> Then, have I reason to be fond of grief? (3.4.93–98)

At this stage in her play, however, she is, like Hamlet, in excessive grief, in continuous memory. The destination of both Hamlet's and Constance's journey in grief is the point where memory is neither painful nor involuntary. They need to reach the state of the speaker in sonnet 30 who uses a kinetic verb to present memory as something over which he has active control: "When to the sessions of sweet silent thought / I *summon* up remembrance of things past." By act 5 we see a calm, reflective Hamlet, able to accept death's place in the life cycle: Yorick's, his father's, or mankind's. He has not stopped remembering; he has stopped grieving.

*Hamlet* presents that most basic of human pains—the moment

when your mind cries out "this cannot be," even as it knows, but refuses to accept, "yes, it is." Hamlet works through denial, anger, and depression before he reaches a state of acceptance.

Death affects our sense of self because it adjusts the coordinates with which we map our world. Consequently we have to renegotiate our relationship to everything and everyone around us. I remember as a child asking my father, when my grandfather had just died, what it was like to lose his father. He said it felt odd to be the oldest generation of his family, suddenly to find himself occupying a different relational position in the world.

Loss is always hard to accept. Hamlet's journey in grief applies to any loss—a theft, the end of a relationship, the death of a public figure or a pet, the amputation of a limb, retirement, menopause, loss of health, the crashing of one's computer hard drive, the relocation of a close friend, or termination of employment. All involve a period of mourning. And the immediate cause of mourning cannot be separated from previous causes of grief. The curious thing about grief is that practice doesn't make perfect. Loss opens up all previous losses, creating one cumulative pain. The death of a loved one revisits every previous moment of vulnerability from childhood onward.

When my father was dying I wrote a series of articles about death in Renaissance literature. My strategy—to write about loss—is also Hamlet's. Hamlet can't put pen to paper because he is dying. But he prevents Horatio from committing suicide because he wants him to relate Hamlet's story: "In this harsh world draw thy breath in pain / To tell my story" (5.2.348–49). The vocabulary of the play's last scene already recasts the events as a literary narrative—the members of the court watch the carnage as "mutes" (the technical term for walk-on actors) or an "audience," Fortinbras has Hamlet borne to a "stage." Hamlet's injunction to Horatio means that the events we have just watched will begin again (indeed, the play we have just watched may already have been Horatio's retelling of the story). Certainly, the play calls attention to its own narrative circularity with a dead/dying character called Hamlet (one a ghost, the other a prince) instructing a loved one (one a son, the other a best friend) to see justice done (in the first instance, "revenge his [father's] most foul and unnatural murder"; in the second, "report me and my cause aright"). Life and art start to merge.

This is because art will help us deal with life and loss. In her poem about loss, "One Art," Elizabeth Bishop tells herself to "write it," to turn her loss into literature. Not everyone can follow this advice. But it doesn't matter because others have already done this for us: we can read; we can go to the theater; we can assuage our pain by watching others handle theirs.

Using literature to process loss is one of the themes of *Titus Andronicus*. In this play Lavinia suffers a series of horrendous losses. She is raped by two men; the rape takes place on the corpse of her husband whom the men have just killed. To prevent her identifying her rapists (and exposing them as the murderers of her husband), the two criminals cut out Lavinia's tongue and amputate both her hands. If Lavinia does not first bleed to death (a concern the play does not address, being not much concerned with realism), she will be unable to speak or write and hence unable to incriminate her violators.

Lavinia is unable to speak about her violation, not because her tongue is amputated but because she feels shame. When her uncle gives her a staff and asks her to guide it with her stumps and write in the sand, she chooses to write *stuprum*. *Stuprum* is the Latin word for shame. It is significant that Lavinia does not use the alternative noun *raptus*, which means theft (and in the Elizabethan period was used to mean abduction of a woman and/or theft of her virginity). And it is significant that she chooses to write in Latin (in a play in which everyone is speaking English, despite the ancient Roman setting). Lavinia cannot voice her experience.

Shakespeare did not invent this cruel plot. (Shakespeare almost never invented a plot, preferring to rewrite stories from earlier authors.) He borrowed it from Ovid's *Metamorphoses*, in which Philomela is raped by her brother-in-law and turned into a nightingale by the gods. (Shakespeare's story, being marginally more realistic than Ovid's, omits the nightingale plot.) In *Titus Andronicus* Lavinia survives the rape and mutilation, opens up a book—Ovid's *Metamorphoses*, as it happens—and turns to the pages about Philomela's rape. Because Lavinia cannot speak, she uses literature to speak for her. Her family recognizes the story and understands what she has endured.

Have you ever noticed how, when you are experiencing personal problems—from divorce to dandruff—you find that same problem featured in every magazine article and newspaper column and billboard advertisement you read? Presumably such problems are regularly featured, but because the situation is now *your* situation, you are alerted to the magazine article's relevance. The same phenomenon applies to literature. If you're in trouble, in misery, seeking comrades or consolation, you find literature has already explored your predicament. It's been written about by Russian novelists, by Japanese poets, by American dramatists, by Roman writers and, of course, by Shakespeare. That is why we read literature: to know that we are not alone; to see how someone else responded in a similar predicament; to hear their expression of our pain.

Like Lavinia we are often speechless, not because we have had our tongue cut out but because our loss is too great to articulate. That is when we need literature to speak for us. We read the story, the poem or the line, again and again until the act of reading has lessened our distress. Dr. Johnson said that the purpose of writing was "to enable the reader better to enjoy life, or better to endure it." In *Titus Andronicus* Shakespeare illustrates the second option.

A year after my father died, a colleague wrote inquiring how I was adjusting to "this new stage of your relationship with your father." I was enchanted by his phrasing. My relationship with my father had not ended; it had entered a new phase. As in literature, endings are beginnings in a different form.

This is true of other kinds of loss such as the loss of something or someone one has never had. Children, for example. In today's two-career-couple culture, many men and women who want a family find they have left it too late to start one; and because the cultural climate tells us that there is no fulfillment comparable to child rearing, and because sophisticated reproductive medicine now exists, further emotional frustrations often follow. At the time one of my friends was facing this, she read a sonnet by a Renaissance woman who was trying to come to terms with her barrenness (the old-fashioned word for infertility). The writer prayed to God to help her find other ways in which to be fruitful. What a wonderful metaphoric approach! In our own twenty-first century lives there are so many ways for people without children (and those with them!) to be "fruitful": caring for neighbors, friends, friends' children, godchildren, colleagues, charity, the community . . . Endings are never endings.

Or, as Ferdinand says in *The Tempest*: "'tis gone. / No, it begins again" (1.2.395–96).

# Epilogue

# WHERE THERE'S A WILL

Shakespeare's century saw the beginning of self-help literature. The sixteenth-century movement known as "humanism," with its interest in cultivating the individual, saw the publication of a flurry of texts designed to help individuals develop their potential. Like today's self-help books, these manuals focused on a specific aspect of personal life. They range from the politically pragmatic—Machiavelli's advice that the ruler *appear* religious, for example—to the physically impossible—Castiglione's instruction that the ideal courtier "be neither extremely short nor tall."

My favorite is the *Galateo* of Giovanni della Casa (1503–56), which enjoyed huge popularity in England after its first English translation in 1576. Della Casa instructs the courtier how (not) to blow his nose: "Nor should you, when you have blown your nose, open your handkerchief and gaze into it, as though pearls and rubies must have descended from your brain."

The quintessential humanist thinker in Shakespeare is Hamlet.

Unlike the medieval Everyman (who acts representatively), Hamlet is defined by his capacity to think *individually*. And what he thinks about is what it means to be human. "What a piece of work is a man, how noble in reason" (2.2.303–4), he tells Rosencrantz and Guildenstern. He agonizes over the fact that humanity can encompass two such different (but related) specimens as his father and his uncle.

The sixteenth century thought and wrote about what it means to be human and how to improve one's behavior and change one's attitudes. There is thus nothing anachronistic about us reading Shakespeare today as self-help literature, for advice about humanity and identity and personal relations.

So what kind of book is this? Is it a self-help book that draws its illustrative material from Shakespeare? Or is it an introduction to Shakespeare in the guise of a genre we all understand: self-help. The answer is: it's both.

We read self-help books for the same reason we read literature. To find solace and inspiration. To find guidance and advice. To find comfort: comfort that we are not alone, that others have shared our experience. Shakespeare and self-help will always overlap.

After Shakespeare my favorite author is Homer. In *The Odyssey* Odysseus recounts his life story to King Alcinous. This lengthy narrative takes up three books, nine through twelve, and book thirteen begins, "Odysseus's story was finished." Here "story" means the narrative of Odysseus's adventures, the events of his life. Later in book thirteen Odysseus invents an elaborate story to conceal his identity. He explains that he is a murderer in exile, providing multiple and specific details to enhance plausibility. The narrative finished, Homer comments, "That was Odysseus's story." "Story" here is a synonym for fiction. *Where There's a Will There's a Way* is a book about stories as fiction and stories as life. There is not much difference between the two. Storytellers from Homer to Shakespeare, and from Shakespeare to Sondheim, have long known this.

I do not invoke Sondheim here just for the alliteration. A few years ago a friend called Eugenie lived with my husband and me. Eugenie is a nun from Burma. She had been brought up in the jungle before entering the convent as a teenager; her order sent her to England to improve her English. One day when I had the flu and was unable to attend the Sondheim musical I had booked for the evening, I asked Eugenie if she would like the theater tickets. "What is theater?" she asked.

What is theater?! I suppose there had been no opportunity—or need—for theater in the jungle or the convent. But what wouldn't I have given to have accompanied Eugenie that evening and witnessed her reaction.

As it happened, she phoned me from the theater foyer at 10:30 p.m. Unable to contain her excitement, unable to wait till she arrived home, she *had* to phone. "Laurie," she exclaimed, "I *love* theater." Then: "Is it a true story?"

From that night on, her appetite for theater, film, video—and for Oxford University Press's series of language learner's classics (classics of English fiction, retold at different linguistic levels to suit five stages of beginner)—was insatiable. And always the same first question: "Is this a true story?" *The Picture of Dorian Gray?*—a true story? *Gulliver's Travels?*—a true story? One day she discovered a video film of *Measure for Measure* (attracted by the picture of the nun on the box). I was dubious about her language ability, to say nothing of her potential reaction to a tale of sexual harassment. I summarized the plot for her. Her reaction: "What a sad story." Then: "Is it true?"

This book is my response to Eugenie's recurrent question. Yes, Eugenie, they are all true stories.

~⁀~

The recurrent theme of this book, as of Shakespeare's plays, is identity: how to find ourselves, how to be true to ourselves, how to relate our sense of identity to others'.

The author of this book has many identities. I was born in Canada but brought up in Scotland, where I was raised in a hybrid Scottish–North American way. If accent is a superficial marker of identity (at least in Britain) I have an identity crisis: my vowel sounds are inconsistent and my idioms are unpredictably British and North American. My mobile phone's ringtone is "Scotland the Brave," but I celebrate Thanksgiving and Labor Day and I wouldn't buy chinos anywhere except Lands' End. Consequently my identity is both and neither: I feel British in North America and North American in Britain.

I didn't start reading Shakespeare until I was twelve. At school Shakespeare was taught as if he were a translation exercise; I remember working through plays line by line, paraphrasing the poetry. That a line's meaning could lie outside its paraphrase—that meaning could reside in tone or attitude, and that tone or attitude could contradict the paraphrase (as when Katherine offers a dutiful speech to Petruchio at the end of *The Taming of the Shrew*) was something I did not realize until much later. Speeches of submission can actually be gestures of defiance (a paradox I like to exemplify in my daily life).

I loved the plays I studied at school but approached them with reverence and trepidation. I didn't see a production of Shakespeare until I was a teenager. In the 1976–77 Royal Shakespeare Company season I saw Judi Dench and Mike Gwilym in *The Comedy of Errors*. To my astonishment and delight there was sex in Shakespeare: Mike Gwilym's Antipholus of Syracuse entered with his neckwear loose, a carnation between his teeth, and a dazed smile, clearly having had a thorough sexual workout with Judi Dench's Adriana (who emerged on her balcony to throw Antipholus her red espadrille as a souvenir). If there was sex in comedy, there was comedy in history. As a schoolchild in Scotland I had read *Richard III* to try to teach myself English history; Alan Howard's Richard III in 1980 offered not a history lesson but a theatrically flamboyant politician (and a poignantly paranoid human being).

And—surprise!—the language wasn't difficult. When you read a play you read speeches; when actors say lines, they utter *thoughts*. When Henry V says, "here comes your father" (5.2.279–80), immediately after he has kissed the princess of France his thought might be "Drat, I'm interrupted just when things are progressing with my girlfriend" (exasperation, frustration) or "My future father-in-law has caught me kissing" (embarrassment, self-consciousness) or "That's over, now back to work" (relief). Long Shakespeare speeches are not set pieces any more than our own utterances are premeditated monologues. A speech of a dozen lines is just a sequence of shorter thoughts in uninterrupted succession. Sometimes the thoughts are punctuated by pauses and silences; like us, Shakespeare characters do not always know what they are going to say (although the actor does!).

A further surprise to me in my early theatergoing days was that the Shakespeare text was a set of suggestions rather than prescriptions. When Duke Frederick interrupted the wrestling match in *As You Like It* (Royal Shakespeare Company, 1982), John Bowe's Orlando protested that he was just warming up ("I beseech your Grace, I am not yet well breath'd"; 1.2.217–18) only to fall flat on his face with exhaustion. Here meaning was clearly *not* content that could be paraphrased!

There is a moment in George Eliot's novel *Middlemarch* when Rosamond Lydgate responds to her husband's revelation of debt with "What can *I* do?" (Eliot's emphasis). Eliot comments, "That little speech of four words . . . is capable by varied vocal inflexions of expressing all states of mind from helpless dimness to exhaustive argumentative perception, from the completest self-devoting fellowship to the most neutral aloofness." As a novice spectator I realized that Eliot's observation applied to plays. How many states of mind can this speech express? How many ways can this line be said? How many ways can this scene be played? Collectively these subsidiary questions form the central question of the literary critic: how many ways can this text have meaning? And that is why I go to the theater again and again. The play is different each time; so are the characters and their decisions.

Shakespeare's most recurrent metaphor is of life as theater. He knew that theater parallels life. Understanding theater can therefore help us understand life. And the process is reciprocal: understanding life can help us understand Shakespeare.

In life we assess what people say, how they say it, why they say it; what they want, what they say they want, what they don't want; what their habits and tics and foibles are, their strengths and weaknesses. We observe their interaction with others. We pay as much attention to their silences as to their utterances. We constantly evaluate textual evidence: people's choice of vocabulary as indicators of tone and attitude ("that's patronizing," we think, or, "that's rather generous"); their euphemisms (are they uncomfortable?); their logic or illogic ("hang on, there's something missing here . . ."); their timing (why did they raise this subject now?); their deviations from their normal attitude (has something changed?). We do this on a daily basis, automatically. There's a technical term for this branch of literary criticism: living.

And if life prepares you to read a Shakespeare play, reading a Shakespeare play prepares you to read life.

As we have seen in this book, Shakespeare's plays are about young love, mature love, creating a good impression, making a marriage, midlife crisis, sexual stereotyping, death, and grief; they are about trust, acceptance, disappointment, risk, and opportunity. How much more relevant does a Renaissance dramatist need to be? A *Complete Works of Shakespeare* is the only guide to life you'll ever need.

So what have I learned from Shakespeare?

- Read between the lines.

- No one can tell you who to be.

- Men feel the same as women.

- Self-reflection leads to self-correction.

- You can't change others, but you can change yourself.

- The ending of our story can always be revised.

- It's not our job to judge others.

- "It is excellent to have a giant's strength but it is tyrannous to use it like a giant" (*Measure for Measure*).

- "Be moderate, be moderate" (*Troilus and Cressida*).

- Little things can become great things.

- Love reappears—again and again.

- If you can't tell the difference between men and women, approach both with caution.

- Have a meal first. (Actually, I learned that from Homer, who is more concerned with practicalities than Shakespeare, but I think it's excellent advice!)

# RELEVANT READING

This is not a bibliography: it is a list of suggestions for related reading—reading related to Shakespeare and to life. I have kept the lists brief. The suggestions are arranged chapter by chapter, and although this results in some degree of overlap, it enables the reader who is reading the book selectively (it's OK, I do the same) to follow up specific issues.

The list for each chapter is divided into two parts. The suggested reading in the first part is for material about contemporary living. An asterisk divides this material from the rest of the list, which contains material about Shakespeare's plays. Where I have thought it helpful to do so, I have followed entries with a parenthetical summary or description of the book's argument.

## CHAPTER 1: IDENTITY
Dunkling, Leslie. *The Guinness Book of Names*. London: Guild Book Publishing, 1974, revised 1986.

Hanks, Patricia, et al. *The Oxford Names Companion*. Oxford: Oxford University Press, 1991, 1998.

*

Barton, Anne. *The Names of Comedy*. Toronto: University of Toronto Press, 1990. (Succinct survey of how dramatists use names from Roman comedy to Shakespeare)

Maguire, Laurie. *Shakespeare's Names*. Forthcoming 2007. (Introductory chapter offers a survey of the link between name and identity across the centuries)

Ryan, Kiernan. *Shakespeare*. 3rd edition. London: Palgrave Macmillan, 2002. (See pages 72–82, "*Romeo and Juliet:* The Murdering Word," for the linguistic dimensions of the tragedy)

Sutherland, John and Cedric Watts. *Henry V, War Criminal? and Other Shakespeare Puzzles*. Oxford: Oxford University Press, 2000. ("What's in a name?" pp. 58–64, discusses *Romeo and Juliet*)

## Chapter 2: Family

Forward, Susan. *Toxic Parents: Overcoming Their Hurtful Legacy and Reclaiming Your Life*. New York: Bantam Books, 1989.

Hendrix, Harville, and Helen Hunt. *Giving the Love That Heals: A Guide for Parents*. New York: Simon and Schuster, 1997.

Neuharth, Dan. *If You Had Controlling Parents*. New York: Harper Collins, 1998.

*

Boose, Lynda. "The Father and the Bride in Shakespeare." *PMLA (Publications of the Modern Language Association of America)* 97: 325–47. (Excellent analysis of the pressure in an early modern family when the daughter gets married)

Foakes, R. A., ed. *King Lear*. Arden 3. London: Thomas Nelson, 1997.

## CHAPTER 3: FRIENDS

Paul, Marla. *The Friendship Crisis: Finding, Making, and Keeping Friends When You're Not a Kid Anymore.* New York: St. Martin's Press, 2004.

Yager, Jan. *When Friendship Hurts: How to Deal with Friends Who Betray, Abandon, or Wound You.* New York: Fireside/Simon and Schuster, 2002.

\*

Carroll, William C., ed. *The Two Gentlemen of Verona.* Arden 3. London: Thomson Learning, 2004. (Good introduction provides a history of friendship literature)

Leggatt, Alexander. *Shakespeare's Comedy of Love.* London: Methuen, 1974. (Chapter 2 on *The Two Gentlemen of Verona* gives this sophisticated play the critical attention it deserves)

Mallette, Richard. "Same-Sex Erotic Friendship in *The Two Noble Kinsmen.*" *Renaissance Drama* 26 (1997): 29–52.

Potter, Lois, ed. *Two Noble Kinsmen.* London: Thomas Nelson, 1997. (Excellent introduction)

## CHAPTER 4: THE BATTLE OF THE SEXES: COMEDY

Gray, John. *Men Are from Mars, Women Are from Venus.* New York: HarperCollins, 1992.

Orlando, Jeannette. *Sexual Harassment in the Workplace: A Practical Guide to What It Is and What to Do About It.* Los Angeles: J. Orlando, 1981.

\*

Parker, R. B. "War and Sex in *All's Well That Ends Well.*" *Shakespeare Survey* 37 (1984): 99–113. (As its title says!)

Riefer, Marcia. "'Instruments of Some More Mightier Member': The Constriction of Female Power in *Measure for Measure.*"

*Shakespeare Quarterly* 35 (1984): 157–69. (Looks at the duke's manipulation of Isabella, and Isabella's consequent loss of voice. Excellent article, reprinted in the revised Signet edition of *Measure
for Measure* [New York, 1988], pp. 153–72)

Rutter, Carol. *Clamorous Voices.* London: The Women's Press, 1988.
(In chapter 2, "Isabella: Virtue Betrayed," actresses Juliet Steven-
son and Paola Dionisotti offer two different Isabellas based on
their Royal Shakespeare Company productions)

Snyder, Susan, ed. *All's Well That Ends Well.* Oxford: Oxford University
Press, 1998. (Introduction covers key issues about Helen and Diana)

## CHAPTER 5: THE BATTLE OF THE SEXES: TRAGEDY

De Becker, Gavin. *The Gift of Fear: Survival Signals That Protect Us
From Violence.* New York: Little, Brown, 1997.

Evans, Patricia. *The Verbally Abusive Relationship.* Holbrook, Mass.:
Adams Media, 1996.

Forward, Susan. *Men Who Hate Women and the Women Who Love
Them.* New York: Bantam Books, 1986.

Kramer, Peter. *Should You Leave?* New York: Penguin, 1997.

NiCarthy, Ginny. *Getting Free: You Can End Abuse and Take Back Your
Life.* Seattle: Seal Press, 1997.

National Domestic Violence Hotline (USA): 1-800-799-SAFE (7233)

*

Dolan, Frances, ed. *The Taming of the Shrew.* Boston: Bedford
Books/St. Martin's Press, 1996. (Reprints a rich array of contextual
material documenting the position of women in the sixteenth
century. A wonderful introduction provides a series of thoughtful
and provocative questions for approaching the play today)

Dusinberre, Juliet. *Shakespeare and the Nature of Woman.* 3rd edition.
London: Palgrave Macmillan, 2003. (Covers Shakespeare's women

throughout the canon, and their historical circumstances, in a series of careful analyses. This book is a fascinating accompaniment to any Shakespeare play that has a female character in it!)

Rackin, Phyllis. *Shakespeare and Women.* Oxford: Oxford University Press, 2005. (Particularly good on *The Taming of the Shrew*—do modern productions tell us more about ourselves than about Renaissance views?—and on the historical context of women)

Schafer, Elizabeth, ed. *The Taming of the Shrew.* Shakespeare in Production series. Cambridge: Cambridge University Press, 2002. (This critical edition covers a stunning array of productions and analyses the history of [interpreting] abuse in performance)

## CHAPTER 6: UNREQUITED LOVE

Halpern, Howard. *How to Break Your Addiction to a Person.* New York: Bantam Books, 1983.

Norwood, Robin. *Women Who Love Too Much.* New York: Simon and Schuster, 1985.

Spezzano, Chuck. *Happiness Is the Best Revenge: Fifty Ways to Let Go of the Past and Find Happiness Now.* New York: Hodder Mobius, 2001.

\*

Zitner, Sheldon P. *All's Well That Ends Well.* London and New York: Harvester Wheatsheaf, 1989.

## CHAPTER 7: ACCEPTANCE

Gray, John. *How to Get What You Want and Want What You Have.* New York: HarperCollins, 1999.

\*

Leggatt, Alexander. "Substitution in *Measure for Measure.*" *Shakespeare Quarterly* 39 (1988): 342–359.

## CHAPTER 8: ANGER

Ellis, Albert, and Raymond Tafrate. *How to Control Your Anger Before It Controls You.* Secaucus, N.J.: Carol Publishing Group, 1997.

\*

Kahn, Coppélia. *Man's Estate: Masculine Identity in Shakespeare.* Berkeley: University of California Press, 1981. (Chapter 1 offers a wonderful study of growing up in *The Taming of the Shrew* and *Romeo and Juliet*, pointing out the lack of outlets for female aggression)

## CHAPTER 9: JEALOUSY

Almonte, Paul, and Theresa Desmond. *Interracial Marriage.* New York: Crestwood House, 1992.

Friday, Nancy. *Jealousy.* New York: M. Evans, 1997.

Malakh-Pines, Ayalah. *Romantic Jealousy.* New York: Routledge, 1998.

\*

Daileader, Celia. *Racism, Misogyny, and the* Othello *Myth: Interracial Couples from Shakespeare to Spike Lee.* Cambridge: Cambridge University Press, 2005. (Excellent cultural assessment of the *Othello* story in literature and in life)

De Sousa, Gerald U. *Shakespeare's Cross-Cultural Encounters.* London and New York: Macmillan and St. Martin's, 1999. (Helpfully intersects gender issues with racial issues)

Kermode, Frank. *Shakespeare's Language.* London: Penguin, 2000. (Pp. 270–83 offer a superb analysis of the language and syntax of suspicion and jealousy in *The Winter's Tale*, which Kermode usefully compares with *Othello*, discussed on pp. 165–82)

Taylor, Gary. *Buying Whiteness: Race, Culture, and Identity from Columbus to Hip-Hop.* London: Palgrave Macmillan, 2005. (An inquiry into the origins of "race" as a category; brilliant and comprehensive)

## Chapter 10: Positive Thinking

Flanagan, Eileen. *Listen With Your Heart: Seeking the Sacred in Romantic Love.* New York: Warner Books, 1998.

Gawain, Shakti. *Creative Visualization.* New York: Bantam, 1978.

Spezzano, Chuck. *Fifty Ways to Change Your Mind and Change the World.* New York: Hodder Mobius, 2002.

Williamson, Marianne. *A Woman's Worth.* New York: Ballantine, 1993.

*

Brooks, Harold F., ed. *A Midsummer Night's Dream.* London: Methuen, 1979. (The introduction is excellent on the role of imagination in the play)


## Chapter 11: Forgiveness

Dosick, Wayne. *When Life Hurts: A Book of Hope.* New York: Harper Collins, 1998.

Dowrick, Stephanie. *Forgiveness and Other Acts of Love.* New York: Norton, 1997.

Kushner, Harold S. *When Bad Things Happen to Good People.* New York: Avon Books, 1981.

Nuckels, Cardwell C., and Bill Chickering. *Healing an Angry Heart: Finding Solace in a Hostile World.* Deerfield Beach, Fla.: Health Communications, 1998.

Smedes, Lewis B. *Forgive and Forget: Healing the Hurts We Don't Deserve.* New York: Pocket Books, 1984.

*

Alexander, Peter, ed. *Pericles.* London: BBC TV, 1984. (As is usual in this series, Henry Fenwick's introduction to the production incorporates useful comments from the cast and director)

Ryan, Kiernan. *Shakespeare.* 3rd edition. London: Palgrave Macmillan, 2002. (Pp. 95–101 deal with suffering in *King Lear*)

Sutherland, John, and Cedric Watts. *Henry V, War Criminal? and*

*Other Shakespeare Puzzles*. Oxford: Oxford University Press, 2000. (Pp. 39–45 [" 'Great thing of us forgot': Albany's Amnesia or Shakespeare's?"] offer an excellent analysis of Shakespeare's imposition of unjust suffering at the end of *King Lear*)

## CHAPTER 12: TAKING RISKS

Bernstein, Peter L. *Against the Gods: The Remarkable Story of Risk*. New York: John Wiley, 1996.

De Mello, Anthony. *Awareness: The Perils and Opportunities of Reality*. New York: Doubleday, 1992.

\*

Cerasano, S. P., ed. *The Merchant of Venice: A Routledge Literary Sourcebook*. London and New York: Routledge, 2004. (Excellent introduction covers mercantile culture and risk in Shakespeare's London; also includes reprints of modern articles on these and other topics, and interviews with actors)

Goddard, Harold. *The Meaning of Shakespeare*. 2 vols. Chicago: University of Chicago Press, 1951. (Now there's a modest book title! Although it's more than fifty years old, most of the chapters in this book have stood the test of time [as evidenced by the fact that the book was reprinted in 2001]. Volume 1, pp. 81–116, deal with *The Merchant of Venice*)

## CHAPTER 13: MATURITY

Kiley, Dan. *The Peter Pan Syndrome: Men Who Have Never Grown Up*. New York: Dodd, Mead, 1983.

Longson, Sally. *Everything You Need to Know About Going to University*. London and New York: Kogan Page, 2003. (Written with the British university system in mind but has lots of transferable advice and questions for the American market)

Rosenberg, Helena Hacker. *How to Get Married After 35.* New York: HarperCollins, 1998.

\*

Alexander, Peter, ed. *Antony and Cleopatra.* The BBC TV Shakespeare. London: BBC Books, 1981. (Pp. 17–28 contain valuable insights from the cast about the characters they play)

Goddard, Harold. *The Meaning of Shakespeare.* (See above under Relevant Reading for chapter 12. Pp. 48–54 deal with the theme of study in *Love's Labour's Lost*)

Steed, Maggie. "Beatrice in *Much Ado About Nothing.*" In *Players of Shakespeare 3,* ed. Russell Jackson and Robert Smallwood. Cambridge: Cambridge University Press, 1993. Pp. 42–51. (Steed talks about playing Beatrice at the Royal Shakespeare Company in 1988. Some very astute observations)

Woudhuysen, H. R., ed. *Love's Labour's Lost.* Arden 3. London: Thomas Nelson, 1998. (Excellent on the topical parody of language in the play)

## CHAPTER 14: LOSS

Brownmiller, Susan. *Against Our Will: Men, Women, and Rape.* New York: Bantam Books, 1976.

Colgrave, Melba, et al. *How to Survive the Loss of a Love.* Los Angeles: Prelude Press, 1991.

De Hennezel, Marie. *Intimate Death: How the Dying Teach Us How to Live.* New York: Vintage, 1998.

Ross, Elisabeth Kübler. *On Death and Dying.* New York: Simon and Schuster, 1997.

\*

Cressy, David. *Birth, Marriage, and Death.* Oxford: Oxford University Press, 1997. (Comprehensive and compellingly readable analysis of three huge topics)

Detmer-Goebel, Emily. "The Need for Lavinia's Voice: *Titus Andronicus* and the Telling of Rape." *Shakespeare Studies* 29 (2001): 75–92. (Analyses the cultural problems of an environment in which it is shameful to speak of rape)

Greenblatt, Stephen. *Hamlet in Purgatory.* Princeton: Princeton University Press, 2000. (Chapter 5 provides sensitive close readings of Catholic/Protestant issues surrounding death in *Hamlet*)

Neill, Michael. *Issues of Death: Mortality and Identity in English Renaissance Tragedy.* Oxford: Oxford University Press, 1997. (Wonderful analyses of Renaissance tragedy—especially *Hamlet* and *Antony and Cleopatra*—in relation to death)